Simply Free
Christ unchains the heart

Gerald O'Mahony

Kevin
Mayhew

First published in 1997 by
KEVIN MAYHEW LTD
Rattlesden
Bury St Edmunds
Suffolk IP30 0SZ

0 1 2 3 4 5 6 7 8 9

ISBN 1 84003 014 3
Catalogue No 1500118

Cover photograph courtesy of Images Colour Library Limited
Cover design by Jaquetta Sergeant
Edited by Peter Dainty
Typesetting by Louise Hill
Printed and bound in Great Britain

CONTENTS

		Page
Introduction		5
1	Images of Freedom	9
2	More Images of Freedom	15
3	The Best Things in Life . . .	21
4	Love Is Free	25
5	Free to Lose All, Free to Gain All	31
6	The Folly of Competition	37
7	The Nature of Love	43
8	Free to Grow	49
9	Responsible Yet Free	55
10	Free and Reconciled	61
11	Free, Still, and Everywhere	67
12	Under a Free Sky	73
13	Freedom of Conscience	79
14	Free from Fear of Death	85
15	Deliver Us from Evil	91

ABOUT THE AUTHOR

Gerald O'Mahony is a Catholic priest, a Jesuit, and the author of many books – on forgiveness, on the Eucharist, on his own life story, on moods and discernment, and most recently on what he calls *The Two-edged Gospel* (Eagle, 1995). Since 1983 he has been working in a retreat house; before that, he taught religion in schools and was then an adviser in religious education.

INTRODUCTION

This introduction, indeed this whole book, is addressed mainly to myself. Sometimes, to God. I speak to myself in the same sort of way as the Psalmist might say, 'Praise the Lord, my soul'; I am saying throughout, 'Thank the Lord, my soul, my self, for the great gift of freedom'. Then, if any others find my words raise an echo in their own hearts, well and good. Well and very good. I have always found that writing about something is my best way of exploring what treasures are there, and though I already appreciate my freedom greatly, there is always more to learn, always more to bring into daily living.

What does it mean, to be free? Are Christians freer than other mortals, and does that make them happier, or more joyful, or more effective, or more persevering than others? What did Jesus bring into human life, what new thing which is still to be found today? Are Christians really free, in any way that would make others wish they could be the same? Have I myself anything that others might dearly wish to share?

My original plan, made many years ago now, was to write a book about Christian detachment, but the word 'detachment' sounded too cold to anyone I tried it out on. Yet there is a detachment from greed, and that kind of detachment puts the whole world and everyone in it into my hands without hurting anybody or anything. To lose the whole world is to gain the whole world; not to grasp with my hands is to learn to possess. The wisdom of Jesus seems to tell of an amazing and desirable power in detachment. The winner is the loser, the loser is the winner. Losing is very easy, so that idea interests me greatly. There is also another very desirable detachment, the detachment from complications, detachment from the tangled web we weave by our weak or sinful dealings. Surely anyone would want to be detached from that web? And Jesus seems to promise a light burden in place of our usual heavy ones. He declared war on those in his time who placed heavy burdens on others instead of helping them. He seems to promise a life uncluttered, a life with ease of heart, a life in which the Christian is not tied down.

Detachment in Christian terms does not mean a coldness of affection. We have only to look at Jesus in his friendships and in his dealings with the sick and the sinful, to see that he is anything but cold. It means rather a singleness of purpose, a readiness to forgo anything that might deflect us from doing the will of God. And the will of God is our salvation, the salvation of all, the rescue of as many as possible, the spread of the kingdom till it covers the whole earth. Perhaps in the meantime that may mean the gospel messenger may have to concentrate on a few disciples when it comes to training for the future, but the ultimate aim is the utmost friendliness and warmth between people and between peoples.

There are always two ways of looking at freedom: freedom *from*, and freedom *to*. Freedom from undesirable things, and freedom to do the desirable. The one needs the other. Simply to be free, with nothing in mind beyond that, leaves a person vulnerable, as Jesus pointed out in his parable about sweeping the house clean and then finding that undesirable elements proceed to move in (see *Matthew 12:44*). But to do what I desire, that needs freedom coming first. A rose in a garden cannot flourish if it is all tangled up in grasses and convolvulus weed. A rose needs space to breathe.

The freedom Jesus brought and brings may be seen first of all in the kind of sicknesses he healed. What was it he set poor people free from? Remember now how he healed the paralysed man who was let down through the roof by the sick man's friends (see *Mark 2:1-12*). He said, 'Son, your sins are forgiven'. That way of speaking meant, in a polite way of speaking about God, 'Son, God has forgiven your sins'. Jesus is the truth. Jesus spoke the truth. The truth will ever set us free, and the truth set the paralysed man free.

Once his sins were forgiven, the man, who had been

completely unable to budge before, quietly got up, picked up his pallet and went home. Jesus has the power, and uses it, to declare sins forgiven, and that gift or that power makes me free. How much there to thank God for, my soul. Sin is the power that tangles us up like flies in a spider's web. But Jesus is stronger, 'the Stronger One'; he has the power to disentangle us from the web, and without hurting our wings.

My favourite picture for freedom is that of the apostle Peter after he has been led out of prison by the angel, thinking he is dreaming but then coming to himself and finding that he really is free *(Acts 12:1-17)*. I have never got over the delight I myself found on discovering that freedom in Christ was not a dream but was a permanent reality. No more chains, no more locked gates, no more brutality that could actually reach me in my innermost self, an open sky, stars above, dawn coming, and friends down the road to whom I could return in freedom.

DEDICATION

For all those whose love has set me free.

CHAPTER 1

Images of Freedom

What does freedom look like, in Gospel terms? Perhaps the best place to start is at the beginning of what is probably the earliest gospel, that of Mark. The first five chapters of Mark, as well as other gospel passages, describe a succession of instances of healing by Jesus of various ailments, but the story is not just about physical ailments. Each of the sicknesses cured has in reality a spiritual counterpart: there is physical paralysis and spiritual paralysis, physical leprosy and spiritual leprosy, and so on. Any reader of the gospels can identify with the sufferer at some level, and seek to find freedom from at least the spiritual ailment in the same way the sufferer in the gospel did.

The key to where the freedom comes from is at the very beginning of Mark's gospel, 'The beginning of the good news of Jesus Christ, the Son of God'. John the baptiser is inviting all and sundry to come and admit they are sinners, and to be baptised as a sign of their wish to be free from sin. Jesus comes to be baptised along with the rest, and hears the voice from heaven saying, 'You are my Son, the Beloved; with you I am well pleased.' He goes away into the desert, driven by the Spirit, and is tempted. When he returns we find him referring to anyone who does the will of God as his brother, his sister or his mother. He is in effect inviting any-one who can believe it to share with him what was spoken to him from heaven. This very invitation once accepted is what makes a Christian and what makes a Christian free.

So with the paralysed man who was let down through the roof to bring him to the attention of Jesus *(Mark 2:1-12)*. Jesus told him his sins were forgiven by God, and called him 'son'. Here too was a son of God and God was well pleased with him in spite of his sins. That which pleased God about him was nothing to do with whether he was weak or strong, a good son or a poor sort of son. He was a son, and on that account God forgave him. So, as it turned out, there was nothing to fear, nothing to keep him glued to his pallet, nothing to fear in the past and therefore nothing to fear in the future. So when Jesus told him to stand up, take his mat and go to his home, the man was able to do so. Not that every paralysed person is so because of being a sinner, but that every sinner is not unlike a paralysed person.

In my first days as a teacher in school or Sunday school, I was too afraid to tell people to believe in God's forgiveness because the whole business of fear and guilt-feelings loomed very large over them and also over me. The sense of freedom came when I realised that God's love is constant, and that I need never be afraid. Nor need I teach others to be afraid. I believe someone counted up the times in the Bible that we are told 'Do not be afraid', and they came to 365! Being released from paralysis does not in fact turn out to be an encouragement to sin again, because once I am no longer afraid of what sin can do to me, it no longer hypnotises me into sinning.

There was, too, a woman who had been suffering from haemorrhages for twelve years, and who had spent all she had on many physicians, only to find herself worse instead of better *(Mark 5:25-34)*. One of the most painful results of her ailment must have been the isolation it imposed on her: being pretty well constantly 'unclean' according to the instructions in the book of Leviticus, she would have had little or no normal social or family life, for fear of having to wash just about everything she touched, and to see to it that even people who touched her were ritually washed clean afterwards. She finally must have elbowed her way through the crowd and touched Jesus' clothes, determined that here at least she could not render him unclean, but that he might heal her.

'Daughter', he called her – daughter of God, sharing his own vision as Son of God. God was well pleased with her, and had been all along. She was God's daughter, 'The Beloved', not 'The Unclean'. So often in our own case too, a failing or bad habit we have had for years, without being able to rid ourselves of it, can be healed by the knowledge that God loves us in spite of it. Suddenly it looms less large on our horizon, and we can cope with it.

Jesus healed a leper *(Mark 1:40-45)*. Reading or hearing the gospel is not likely to heal leprosy today except indirectly (as for example by inspiring doctors, researchers, nurses), yet there is a form of spiritual leprosy which it does heal. Indeed I am convinced that the gospels were written to bring to our eyes and ears the spiritual healing and freedom first of all, with the physical healings as parallels and examples. Jesus wanted no one to be excluded from the community. Anyone, no matter what their condition, could come up to Jesus and ask to be admitted to his company. He touches the leper, stretches out his hand and touches him, chooses to touch him.

In spiritual terms, none need feel themselves lepers because of what they have done or failed to do: God welcomes them as much as anybody, if they want to belong to God. There is also a shyness and feeling of inadequacy amounting to a spiritual leprosy, which many people feel, for instance, on entering a room full of strangers. We can feel that everyone else is better than us, more at home, everyone else belongs while we are the stranger. In the case of some people, they feel this isolation nearly all the time, as if everyone else belongs upon the face of the earth, while they alone do not seem to fit in. I feel that way myself at times. Then is the time to remember Jesus and the leper. I can make myself one with the leper, and let Jesus touch me with his hand, inviting me into the circle. 'You are as precious as any of them, so feel free and at home: come on in.'

When in Mark's gospel Jesus drives out 'unclean spirits',

there can be little doubt that what the gospel writer is talking about is mental illness *(Mark 1:21-28)*. There is a connection between the way Jesus sets out teaching in the synagogue in Capernaum 'with authority', straight from what he knew in his heart from his Father and not from someone else's books, and the way he can free the sufferer from mental illness on the same occasion. It was the books that had got the poor man thoroughly mixed up, more than likely. The other big example given early on in Mark is the case of the poor demented man who had a 'Legion' of unclean spirits in his head *(Mark 5:1-20)*. In our own measure, we can all suffer from being pulled in a thousand directions by opposing plans and by fears of doing the wrong thing, no matter what we plan to do. Jesus can give us, as he gave that poor man, one simple way ahead: I am God's child; God will love me whichever way I decide to go forward, so I need not panic. I can sit peacefully at Jesus' feet.

The healing of blindness and deafness has all sorts of meanings, but I could pick out just one or two meanings here. The central question about hearing, hinted at always in the healing of deaf people, is whether I can hear God saying to me, 'You are my beloved child; I am well pleased with you', even though I am aware of myself as a sinner or at the very least weak and wilful. First comes the ability to trust that God is saying those words to Jesus; then comes the ability to trust Jesus when he applies those same words to me, even though I am definitely unworthy. Hearing the words and trusting that they apply to me sets me free from all the negative words that my own memory and imagination imposed on me before, and try to impose on me evermore. The words of God are gentle words, the still small voice of calm, words that come into my heart like a drop of water entering quietly, gently and sweetly into a sponge.

Freedom from blindness has much the same meaning as freedom from deafness: it means seeing reality as it is, and not living with lies or illusions. If I can see in Jesus the chosen

Son of God, and if I can then trust that he is right when he says I am a chosen son or daughter of God, then all the false self-images begin to fall away. It means letting go of the enormous effort of trying to please God or achieve any kind of perfection by my own strength, since a perfection greater than any I could achieve is there for the simple believing. Then the rest of my life can be spent in gratitude to God, because now my eyes are seeing straight. Like Bartimaeus who used to be blind, instead of going my own way I follow Jesus on the Way *(Mark 10:46-52)*.

Very often under stress we can feel like the poor woman who was bent double *(Luke 13:10-17)*, unable to see the beauty of the sky and the clouds above us, or the distant mountains, or the trees or the love and concern in other people's eyes. The promise of Jesus, that we may regard ourselves in truth as God's children, enables us to straighten up, resume our own dignity, leave God to carry the sky, and ourselves to walk freely under it. I remember hearing this attitude of over-anxiety called 'the Atlas complex', as if the universe would cave in unless I continue to carry the sky on my back, like the mythological giant who lived in the Atlas mountains.

The epileptic boy *(Mark 9:14-29)* reminds me of the way I can have sudden lapses from virtue, suddenly break my promises or good resolutions and reveal my underlying weakness. Jesus speaks about the necessity of prayer to combat this one: we must pray if we hope to withstand temptation. But at least the remedy is there, and we can even see from the example of Peter and the other apostles that forgiveness is there as well if in spite of Jesus' warnings we do not pray.

I need not fear being lost, losing my way in life, since Jesus like the shepherd will come and find me *(Luke 15)*. If I am in the right place, like the ninety-nine sheep or the coins safe in the woman's purse or like the elder brother of the lost boy, then all is well; if I am lost, like the one sheep or the one coin, or the boy, then God will come and find me, so all will be well. Much better to stride out and use the freedom my owner gives me, than to let fear of doing the wrong thing by accident paralyse me.

I need not greatly fear getting wounded, since Jesus my Good Samaritan will come and rescue me *(Luke 10:29-37)*. I need not fear my own weakness *(Mark 14:38)*, since Jesus will forgive me and always, always give me another chance.

These and such as these are the images of freedom the gospels give us for our consideration and our comfort and strength. This kind of freedom we may ask for with confidence.

CHAPTER 2

More Images of Freedom

There are more ways of being free than simply being free from sickness. So also there are more ways of being free suggested in the Bible. Some of them are in the gospels again, some in St Paul or other places in the New Testament, and many are in the Old Testament. One of the most intriguing places in the gospels is that in which the collectors of the temple tax came to Peter and asked whether his teacher did not pay the temple tax *(Matthew 17:24-27)*. When Peter took this problem to Jesus, Jesus asked him, 'From whom do kings of the earth take toll or tribute? From their children or from others?' When Peter said, 'From others', Jesus said to him, 'Then the children are free'. None the less he asked Peter to go fishing, and to pay the tax for both of them. God would provide.

This story reflects Jesus' way of balancing the fact that he is the Son of God, and therefore has no need to pay taxes concerning God's house; and on the other hand he is the Servant, who has emptied himself of the divinity in so far as that is possible. In other words, he does not claim any privileges before God although he has every right to do so. And here in this passage from Matthew he is including Peter and indeed all his disciples in the same process: Peter strictly speaking has no need to pay the taxes, but he is not to give himself airs on that account. A present-day disciple has strictly speaking no need to pay taxes of any kind to God: God will love the disciple anyway, since the disciple is also a child of God's. But although we have the right to pay no taxes, we are encouraged not to trade on our close relationship with God, but to do our utmost to aid the cause of Jesus in the modern world.

St Paul uses the image of adoption: 'You did not receive a spirit of slavery to fall back into fear, but you have received a spirit of adoption' *(Romans 8:15)*. Parents who adopt a child have always wished to show no favouritism; they will love the adopted one as much as they love their own child or children. Christians who can worthily or unworthily say to God, 'I am your beloved child; with me you are well pleased', can be sure that God loves them as dearly as he loves his own Son. What we are freed from is slavery and fear. St John adds another ingredient: 'The slave does not have a permanent place in the household; the son has a place there for ever. So if the Son makes you free, you will be free indeed' *(John 8:35f)*. Part of the fear which our adoption as children frees us from is the fear that God might change his mind. Once we are children, we are children for ever. The original knowledge and vision was Jesus', but he has shared it with any who will believe him.

This does not mean that we will never sin again. But it does give us eagles' wings, to keep going tirelessly, to recover instantly each and every time we sin. Our sins become like wounds inflicted in the battle of life, and we refuse to be laid low by them. We acknowledge our weakness, ask for forgiveness knowing that it is already given, and we carry on trying to do good and be good. A slave would be conscious all the time that the score was mounting up against him, and that the day of reckoning was getting ever closer. This ability of the child to get up and try again must be one of the things Jesus had in mind when he said that 'the one who believes in me . . . will do greater works than these [that I do]' *(John 14:12)*. Jesus himself never had the sickening task of realising his own sin and then getting straight up and trying all over again to love God, but this is the power he gives to his brothers and sisters.

The Old Testament is teeming with images of freedom which are taken up in the New Testament and applied to the freedom which is ours by virtue of believing we are sisters or brothers of Christ. The darkness of night and storm and imprisonment is contrasted with the dawn of light and the peace and brightness after the storm and the bliss of freedom from confinement. Jesus speaks often of the blindness of his enemies, whose eyes are so full of their own virtues that they can no longer see their own limitations as mortal beings. Then there is the freedom from slavery in Egypt, one of the memories of the people, a memory they tried never to forget. In Christian terms this is the slavery to the rules and regulations which human law-makers are so liable to pile up and load onto the shoulders of others. With this kind of slavery comes the deadly fear that if I cannot keep all the rules, God will cease to love me, or even worse, that God still loving me will regretfully consign me to the outer darkness because of my poor performance. Jesus was always, always simplifying, until he finally got it all down to just one rule which none of us can ever fully keep anyway: 'This is my commandment, that you love one another as I have loved you' *(John 15:12)*. The love Jesus showed us and shows us is everlasting, and is not conditional on my performance.

The crossing of the Red Sea or the Reed Sea is remembered for its finality: there was no more pursuit, the freedom was total. That is why Christians link that memory to the celebration of baptism, the celebration that here is a child of God, a slave no longer, and never again to be held by the tentacles of that slavery. The crossing of the wanderers over the Jordan and into the Promised Land is another water crossing, enriching the former crossing. From now on the one who had no land has a land of her own, the one who had no husband has a husband who will love her for ever, no matter what she does, and the one who had no family has a family rooted in the beginnings of time and before. When troubles come, no matter how serious, there will always be a rebuilding, always a coming home again at last. The 'everlasting' side of the promises took a long time to be understood, and was only finally fixed in the life and death and resurrection of Jesus. Jesus on the cross forgiving his enemies showed us and shows us God's love completely unquenchable. He would never turn away anyone who asked for pity and remembrance, no matter how wicked the performance might have been and no matter how unable the sinner was to promise to do better in future (see *Luke 23:34-43*).

Another beautiful change of emphasis brought about by Jesus is the change from the priority of 'the people' to the priority of 'the least of the little ones'. If the least of the little ones cannot keep up with the rest of the people of God, then God will send the people back to pick up the lost one. If the whole Church sailed away happily into heaven and left me behind, then Jesus would be with me, the least one, and the others would have to come back for us. Wherever the Bible says things like, 'I will never forget you, my people', I can legitimately transfer it to say to me, 'I will never forget *you*, the least of my little ones'. This unique relationship which each of us is given means that any one of us is like an independent state, like a walled city with its own well inside the walls. The Christian Church is the company of those who know themselves to be individually precious to God their Father, and who wish to support one another in this belief besides spreading it as widely as the human race.

There is freedom from drought, since the living water is always springing up within the city walls of each of us. There are no extremes of heat or cold, since the Spirit of God cools the heat and warms the cold. Neither are there extremes of emotion, since God speaks with a still, small voice which encourages the downhearted and warns the over-excited to let God do the work. There are no barriers, since now the one who seeks God need no longer go to Jerusalem, find the temple, enter the court of the Gentiles, then qualify to enter the court of the Jewish women, then qualify to enter the court of the Jewish men, then the Holy Place where only the priests could go, then go through the curtain to the Holy of Holies and the presence of God, where only the High Priest or his representative could go. The curtain is torn, and any child of God, male or female, gentile or Jew, can enter freely.

A Christian is free even from death, in that death for a Christian is changed into something not to be feared any more. My relationship with God is one of faith, and faith can move mountains, even the mountain of death. There is God, and here am I, and there is a mountain in between; but the mountain will crumble before God's love for me shows any signs of crumbling. My Master has conquered death, because reliable people in our tradition have seen him alive after he was crucified, and not just people of his own generation: reliable people of our tradition in my own day have seen him alive and well and indestructible. He is the anchor fixed in eternity and yet chained to us in love and kinship: one day we too will go ashore in safety.

CHAPTER 3

The Best Things in Life . . .

When I was a little boy of five years or so, my parents had an old wind-up gramophone in a polished wooden cabinet. The sound-horn wound downwards and came out from the middle of the cabinet, rather than up on top. I used to work my way through all their old 78 rpm records from the 1920s and 1930s which they no longer had the time to play, what with the three of us children. One of my favourites was a song whose theme has stayed in my memory and indeed in the public imagination: 'The best things in life are free.' It was sung on our record by a duo, Layton and Johnstone, both of them singing and Turner Layton being the pianist. The words (from memory) were

> The sun belongs to everyone,
> the best things in life are free.
> The stars belong to everyone,
> they gleam there for you and me.
> The flowers in spring,
> the robins that sing,
> the moonbeams that shine,
> they're yours, they're mine;
> And love can come to everyone:
> the best things in life are free.

Freedom is not just a question of being free from the past and free from present worries, but also a question of whether the things in front of me are free for the taking, or are they denied to me or restricted in some way? A Christian believes and celebrates and acts on the belief that we are

21

children of God who created and owns everything, and that therefore everything we see is our inheritance, to be cherished because it will be ours one day. In a sense, all God has is ours already, as the father says to the elder son in Jesus' story of the younger son who ran away and came back *(Luke 15:31)*. What the song says about all the best things in life being free has a special meaning for Christians.

The philosopher Bishop Berkeley had a way of looking at reality which has always appealed to me deeply: it is almost as if God has created the universe separately for each being that looks out on the world and the sky. No one else possesses my world, which I can see from my unique point of view. Even someone standing beside me sees a different scene, even if only slightly different at that moment. The only one who sees exactly what I see without my having to point things out . . . is God. God and I share my world, and no one else does. And God, for a Christian, is 'Abba, my Father', and completely friendly, incurably so. God may not always like what I am doing, but God always likes me.

This way of looking at life can be the cure for greed. If we think of children playing a game of Ludo, they have a choice: either to play to win and be disgusted if they lose, or to sit loosely to the game and enjoy the ebb and flow of fortunes no matter who is winning. The whole game is mine, the whole game belongs to all four players so long as they do not insist on grabbing the whole game for themselves. God creates one world and one universe, and it belongs to everyone so long as they do not try to grab it for themselves. When I see the abandon with which some people pick wild flowers, I thank God that the stars are still out of reach. All the stars are mine already, so why should I try to pluck them out of anyone else's universe?

'Blessed are the meek, for they will inherit the earth' *(Matthew 5:5)*. If like Jesus we do not go to pieces when someone takes our earth away from us, it is because we know the whole earth and heaven as well is ours already, and my persecutors are the ones who are limiting their prospects to exactly what they take from me and no more. 'He who binds to himself a joy, doth the winged life destroy; he who kisses a joy as it flies, lives in Eternity's sunrise', as was said so beautifully by the poet William Blake. To know myself as God's beloved child gives me and any Christian a perspective point, a view point, from which to view the whole of reality from the exact spot from which God views my world. I then view the world as the beloved son or daughter of the one Jesus refers to in many images in the teachings and parables: the king who had a son to be married *(Matthew 22:2)*, the owner of the vineyard *(Luke 13:6-7)*, the father waiting for one son to come home and for the other son to have a change of heart *(Luke 15:20, 28)*, the owner of the flock of sheep *(John 10:29* and *Ezekiel 34:6)*, the landowner *(Matthew 20:1-16; 13:24)*, the first source of all light *(John 8:12-16)*, the first source of all power *(John 17:2; Matthew 28:18)*, the owner of the treasury *(Matthew 17:27)*, the end of the way *(John 14:6)*. My elder brother tells me to count myself as sharer of his inheritance as the first-born . . . indeed in my own personal world-vision I *am* the first-born, as is any Christian *(Hebrews 12:23)*.

And as we come into our Promised Land we find 'a land with fine, large cities that you did not build, houses filled with all sorts of goods that you did not fill, hewn cisterns that you did not hew, vineyards and olive groves that you did not plant' *(Deuteronomy 6:10f)*. My own world has been the result of millions upon millions of years of work on the part of God, and thousands upon thousands of years of work on the part of my human ancestors.

There is a parable of Jesus which invites me to identify with a man who owed ten thousand talents *(Matthew 18:23-35)*, billions of pounds in today's money, a sum totally unpayable by one individual. If God was to call in the debts (which will not be called in as long as I forgive my own debtors), then I would be totally incapable of paying God back: for the sun, for the moon, for the stars, for the earth under my feet and the laws of gravity that keep it there; for the birds and plants and the winds and the sea and the lakes and the rivers; for the animals and for my fellow human beings; for my parents and the love that has been shown me by so many people for so many years; for my eyes and my ears and all my senses, for the power to walk and run and speak and sing, for the joy of learning to do things and the treasures of memory. All of this, and so much more, is beyond the price of however many billions of pounds and has been given to me without my having to pay for it. The only way I could ever pay for my pair of eyes is with another pair of eyes . . . or with the same pair of eyes, given back to the owner in willing service.

I honestly think that standing in the presence of God I have no rights at all to anything, since everything I can imagine or see is a gift from God. Yet the same God invites me to think of myself as his child forever, and all these gifts as my inheritance – again, so long as I am willing to let my sisters and brothers have their inheritance. If I start to grasp and grab, then I show that I have in no way understood that all this is in fact my inheritance, and thus I am back in my slavery and indebtedness.

So the little song with which I started this chapter awakes endless echoes for a Christian. St Paul puts it all this way: 'For all things are yours, whether Paul or Apollos or Cephas or the world or life or death or the present or the future – all belong to you, and you belong to Christ, and Christ belongs to God' *(1 Corinthians 3:22f)*. You are mine, and I am yours, my fellow creature, so long as we do not try to possess one another.

CHAPTER 4

Love Is Free

Remembering that little song, 'The best things in life are free', I have mentioned already the free gifts of nature, the likes of the robins and moonbeams in the song. Time now to look at the last lines of the song: 'And love can come to everyone . . . the best things in life are free.' How free is love? Certainly when love comes our way we are very conscious of it as a gift. When some good person is revealed as loving us, we almost always feel very humble as a result. But there are other people who make us earn their love. From such people love is anything but free: we have to pay dearly for their love. And what about the many people in the human race who feel that no one really loves them, no matter how hard they try to earn some love?

At the heart of our Christian belief is the firm trust that God is love, and that God loves each of us always, even if nobody else does. Someone once pointed out to me that when St Paul gives his famous description of love (in *1 Corinthians 13:4-8)*, we can equally well put in 'God' where Paul writes 'love', since God is love. The result gives a fresh way of looking at Paul's words. *God is patient and kind.* From my window I can see a huge old tree, probably two hundred years old. How patient God is, waiting for creatures to grow in their own time. And all through the years, God's regard for the tree has been kindly. For me, too, God will wait patiently, and always with the kindest of interest. Even if I fail in goodness seventy times seven times in the day, God will never lose patience with me: I can always start again, try again. I do not have to pay for his love by my success in goodness.

We are thinking here of the Father of Jesus Christ, the One we know as the First Person of the Trinity. *God is not boastful or arrogant or rude.* If I had created the sun, the moon and the whole universe of suns and moons and all the things that exist on them, and all the beauties of our world and all the laws that govern the movements of the planets and their seasons, I would be forever nudging people and pointing out to them how wonderful the whole creation is. God on the other hand is so modest about creation that half the human race does not believe God exists at all! The prophets may ask for praise to be given to God, but they do so on behalf of God who is himself silent on the subject. Again, the prophets may call the rest of us ungrateful wretches, but God himself is unfailingly courteous. God never rubbishes us (as the current phrase has it), but is always thinking high thoughts about his children: 'You are my beloved daughter; you are my beloved son.'

Hence also, *God is not envious.* Why indeed should God ever be envious of our performance? God is love, and wherever love is found, God is only too delighted. There can never be too much of love. *God does not insist on his own way.* The One who could obliterate us at any moment is so courteous that he takes each day from where we left it yesterday. God picks up the pieces of whatever we have smashed in our weakness or ignorance or downright malice, and slowly but firmly begins to turn it into something even better than what was there in the first place. The sin of Adam and Eve was turned into a 'happy fault', as the old hymn says, when Christ died on the tree of life.

God is not irritable or resentful. God does not take offence, so we need not be scrupulous or over-worried, thinking that God is still brooding about some fault of yesterday. God starts each day fresh with each one of us. He is not building up a head of steam ready for a great explosion. The still small voice always is, always was and always will be small and still. The action of God is ever like a drop of water entering gently, sweetly and quietly into a sponge, with any person of good will. Jesus made it clear that human tragedies like blindness or like a tower falling on people walking past underneath are not punishments. The tower fell because it was badly constructed or in a state of decay, not because God was resentful towards the poor unfortunates underneath.

God does not rejoice in wrongdoing, but rejoices in the truth. As far as any Christian is concerned, Jesus is the truth. One of Jesus' central statements is contained in the story of the Prodigal Son in Luke's Chapter Fifteen. So God rejoices in that story, as being a true reflection of his own attitudes. God loves the sinner all through the time the sinner is sinning, but is longing all the time for the sinner to turn back and come home, in whatever state of disarray. There are good things God likes us to be doing, and wrong things he hates us to be doing, but us he loves equally, either way. And of course God could never share the morbid delight humans are capable of, in hearing or reading about dreadful actions someone else has done. The general public may like to read about degrading events in the news, but the parents of the people concerned are not among the gloaters. God has for us a parent's love.

God bears all things. He is always ready to excuse us and to put up with our foibles and indeed our madness at times. *God believes all things,* even to believing we his children are beautiful when we have ceased to believe it ourselves. *God hopes all things,* even when to all appearances there is no longer room for hope. *God endures all things,* and his strength, his patience never snaps. God is the one and only Rock that nobody and nothing can shift from the attitude of love. *God who is love never ends.* God's love for each one of us will still be there when the mountains have crumbled into dust.

I have also heard this passage from First Corinthians described as being a portrait of Jesus. Well, if God is love and Jesus is God, God the Son and Second Person of the Trinity, then we can see what happens when we replace the word 'love' by the word 'Jesus'. *Jesus is patient.* We can see his patience in the gospels, and he is the same yesterday, today and forever. He was patient unto death, always countering human ignorance with further ways of saying the truth, and always countering human hatred with a shield of the truth. His disciples tried his patience, and his enemies even more so, but Jesus was always compassionate to the crowds. *Jesus is not envious*, since like his Father he knew already that everything that is good was his already. We could share the same peace of mind if we only could see the whole universe and heaven itself as our inheritance.

Jesus is not boastful or arrogant or rude. He never boasts except in God his Father. Being the greatest of the prophets, he is entitled to point our attention to the greatness of his Father in a way that his Father never does. Mary speaks in a similar way in her Magnificat, speaking only of the great things God has done for her, not anything that she herself has done. Indeed we are told that Jesus in the resurrection asked politely what things the two disciples were discussing on the road to Emmaus, quite as if the events had happened to someone else. Jesus was straight with his opponents, giving as good as he got, and better, but it was always for their own good, a jolt to shake their complacency. The spirit of God is gentle where it finds good will, but implacable where it finds an opposing wind coming against it, the wind of anti-love.

Jesus was only intolerant with the intolerant, only unforgiving with the unforgiving, because he stood for the God of forgiveness. His opponents had only to turn and forgive, to be forgiven. The only time Jesus gave physical expression to anger was to expel those who were putting a price on God's love, in their buying and selling in the temple.

Jesus does not insist on his own way, but takes us as he finds us, using that as a starting point. He did not insist that the woman at Jacob's well should sort out her married life before speaking with her and dealing gently with her. He did not tell the five thousand strong crowd to go home again because they were interrupting what was to have been a quiet time with his disciples in a lonely place. *Jesus is not irritable or resentful.* He seems to be able to tolerate any amount of inconvenience and rough-and-ready treatment from the crowds, calling them 'sheep without a shepherd' who have need of him. So far from harbouring resentment or revenge in his heart, he prayed for forgiveness for his very murderers.

Jesus does not rejoice in wrongdoing. When he forgives, he adds, '. . . from now on do not sin again', even though he will forgive again if the sinner sins again. *Jesus rejoices in the truth* as he did over each and every sinner who repents, and as he did when rejoicing that God hides his wonders from the wise and intelligent and reveals them to infants. *Jesus bears all things, believes all things, hopes all things, endures all things*, for the sake of his little ones. He gathers us under his wings, and fiercely resists any attempt to take us away from him. *Jesus never ends*, but is, was and always will be the perfect mirror of God who is love.

Whichever way we look at the question, love is certainly free. God's love is there for the asking; whenever I can say 'Now', God is already loving me and forgiving me.

CHAPTER 5

Free to Lose All, Free to Gain All

We are all free to lose the kingdom of this world, and to gain the kingdom of God. The best modern way of expressing 'the kingdom of God' that I have ever come across is 'living in God's way' (in Alan T. Dale's book *New World*). 'The kingdom of God is like this . . .' becomes 'Living in God's way is like this . . .'. It involves acknowledging God (the First Person) as monarch, as owner of all, as the only source of light and true power, the only source of love, the only One who loves without having been loved first (and who therefore makes no pre-conditions when loving us), the Rock not based on any other rock. Jesus is our Teacher about the One he calls his Father, the Father who himself has no mother or father, no outside source. Jesus' way involves letting God have things God's way, since to go with God is to go with our own true grain, and to go with God is to go with the wind of the Holy Spirit.

Some of the teachings of Jesus he tells us are necessary; others are voluntary. 'Unless you change and become like children, you will never enter the kingdom of heaven' *(Matthew 18:3)*. That one is necessary. It is clearly some kind of gateway into living in God's way. St Ignatius of Antioch, writing only seventy years after the death of Jesus, has a beautiful and succinct phrase: for human beings 'faith is the beginning and love is the end' (in his *Letter to the Ephesians*, 14). God loves me; when I believe God loves me, then my life in God's way begins. After that my belief and my trust grow into loving others. This is the faith which justifies us, the faith which is more fundamental than any good deeds I could come to perform *(see e.g. Galatians 3:1-9)*.

This necessary 'becoming like a little child' means handing over the reins of my life to God as a little child takes the hand of an adult before crossing a dangerous road. I have to admit that I am not the source of love and light and power, that I am not a monarch in my own small kingdom, that my universe is mine by gift and not by right. And this I can do once I realise that God is love and God is unfailingly loving towards me. This is necessary for us, but at the same time it is free in that it is something we can do: it is only a question of letting go of the notion that we can find eternal life on our own. Everyone is bound to come face to face with their own basic helplessness at the hour of death, but Jesus wants us to face it from the start and to enrich our lives beyond recognition as a result.

Faith or trust is a gift from God, but a gift that I can let happen or not let happen. Love, the power to love God in loving others, is a gift that follows on faith, but love is a gift I have to pray for, since it involves voluntary effort and God does not take it for granted that I want to love to the maximum. For a Christian, the central motive for living a good and selfless life is gratitude, gratitude to God for countless gifts and personal favours received and endless gifts promised and guaranteed. Ignatius of Antioch has another revealing observation when he refers to faith as 'the flesh of the Lord' and love as 'the blood of Jesus Christ' (*To the Trallians*, 8). The one always comes before the other in our Eucharist, and whereas the bread of the Eucharist is always comforting, the wine of the Eucharist is both stimulating and challenging. God comforts me, then invites me to respond.

The initial gateway, the initial surrender of faith is immensely rewarding as soon as the step is taken, whereas love can stay painful for the rest of human life. With the gift of faith to know myself loved by the God of the universe dwelling in me, being loved as much as the favourite child . . . I find myself free from slavery to false notions of God, such as that he would ever send me to hell at the same time as loving me; free from slavery to anxiety and scruples about whether I have done things properly. In my own case that was a liberation from eighteen years of torture. The surrender means freedom from fear of judgement, from the need to pretend, from despair, from the need for success, from dithering whether to do this rather than that; freedom from slavery to religious rules and regulations (and indeed from slavery to any kind of rules and regulations). Wonderful to be free from worrying about what other people think of me, free from having to fix people and put them right or judge them; free from regrets, free from competition, free from needing praise all the time. All these things it was a pleasure to trade in, in return for finding my self-worth only in God.

'Detachment', then, really means not letting any of these horrors get a hold of me ever again. It has nothing to do with being cold or miserable. On the contrary, as long as a person is consumed by anxiety, that person can never give whole-hearted love to anyone else, whereas one who is protected from anxiety by trust in the Good News has a whole free heart to love with. Spiritual books sometimes tell us we should be 'indifferent' about the joys and pleasures and sorrows of this world, and this word too needs to be understood. It does not mean that we are expected by our religion to have a 'couldn't care less' attitude or a cold attitude to the ups and downs of our daily lives. What it does mean is that if anything in my life is getting me back into the realm of slavery such as I have been describing, then I should resist the alien force with all my might, chiefly by prayer.

There is a beautiful prayer which has survived the changes of the centuries. It comes in the Eucharist between the offering of the bread and that of the wine. A little water is dropped into the chalice and a translation of the centuries-old version of the prayer would run like this: 'God, in a wonderful way you created and gave dignity to human nature, then in an even more marvellous way renewed it. Grant that by the mystical union of this water and wine we may be made partakers of the divinity of Jesus, who has deigned to become sharer in our humanity.' Water there is seen as the 'human' element, and wine as the 'divine', in the same way as in the story of the marriage feast at Cana *(John 2:1-11)*, where Jesus is proclaiming his mission of changing the human (water) into the divine (wine).

The idea of the prayer is very simple. Jesus traded in his divinity, so that we could trade in our humanity. Each in the end retains what was traded in, but the new creature in our case is infinitely enriched. We can learn to live in God's way.

There is something utterly touching about the thought of Jesus literally becoming a little child in order to take on our humanity. We have to do something similar to learn God's way of living, but the gains are infinite in our case. God in Jesus is more or less saying, 'Unless I became a little child, I could not enter the kingdoms of the world.' And what a long process it was for Jesus: not just his babyhood, which we often think about, but also his thirty or so years to the day when he began his public life. His prayers and hymns and the stories and poems that he comes out with in his public teaching all imply years and years of observation.

He was a carpenter, but I cannot think of any references to carpentry in his teachings. But what a rich world is there in the teachings: farmers, landowners, reapers, foxes, hens and chicks, thieves, stewards, weddings, children playing weddings and funerals, bridesmaids, servants, shepherds, lost sheep, women grinding corn, women baking, widows, lost coins, broken-hearted parents, kings and armies going to war, soldiers demanding to have their baggage carried, different kinds of trees, people going to law, travellers, travellers being attacked by brigands, problems over house security, blind people being led by the sighted, wild flowers in the fields, wild birds flying above. Almost any situation one can think of, Jesus either went there or spoke about it in a way that showed he knew it in his own life.

I remember seeing a television film of the life of Jesus many years ago now. Jesus was pouring out his speeches and sayings at top speed, and as if he had only just thought of them. Perhaps there was some valid dramatic point in representing him like that, as if to say he knew there was not much time left for him to get his message across. But it seems much more likely that Jesus spent his 'hidden life' gradually crafting his sayings and stories. The poem of the Beatitudes or the poem (for such it undoubtedly is) about 'Ask and you shall receive' or the story of the Prodigal Son must surely have been designed long before. By a happy coincidence the word for carpenter in the Greek, the language of the gospels, is the same as the word for a poet. Both are 'makers'.

If Jesus had to spend thirty years becoming a little child and then following the years through to adulthood, surely we should not expect to learn divinity overnight. I have out-lined some of the beautiful freedoms that come from letting God's love be my lode-star, but there are many disappoint-ments along the way, as we try to live completely in God's way. We find that our own earthy ways reassert themselves, and we have to accept forgiveness all over again, to try a fresh start. Jesus even as an adult was forever putting his hand in God's as if he were still a little child. He wanted only to do what he heard his Father asking, as he looked to his conscience and his knowledge of his Father in one situation after another.

A few times in my life I have had holidays sailing, up and down English rivers and sometimes out to sea. My compan-ions and I discovered the wisdom of sailing out for the day against the wind or against the tide, if it meant we would have the wind and tide with us coming home. We would know then how to time the day and get back to make the supper at a reasonable hour. The turnabout in the afternoon was always dramatic. We had been labouring and tacking this way and that to make headway against the wind, and the sea or the river water was splashing liberally into the boat, rocking and jarring all within. Then as soon as we turned about to come home, it seemed as if the wind had disappeared and there was a sudden calm. The wind was the same in fact, but we were just going with it instead of against it. That to my mind is a fine illustration of what it feels like in our human lives each time when we do the about turn and look on ourselves again as children of a God we can trust. All the turmoil and conflict seems to disappear as if it never existed, deep down all is calm. What we have done is to stop forcing our way against the Spirit of God; instead we have turned round to go with the Spirit, whose presence we can recognise by the peace and tranquillity which comes over us. We can tell then that this is what we were first created for, and what has been even more marvellously restored to us.

CHAPTER 6

The Folly of Competition

What I have mentioned as 'the Atlas complex' is a disease, one of the main causes of panic in our lives. One of the main causes of the Atlas complex is the spirit of competition. We feel that all others, or at least some people in particular, are getting ahead of us in the race towards God and heaven, or, what comes to the same thing, in the race towards perfect fulfilment as a human being. Taking on the notion of life as a race towards God can turn us into self-righteous beings, into pretenders, or tip us into the depths of despair. Either way, competition for the favours of God is a blind alley, a dangerous road.

What then of St Paul, when he writes things like this: 'Do you not know that in a race the runners all compete, but only one receives the prize? Run in such a way that you may win it' *(1 Corinthians 9:24)*? Elsewhere Paul says, 'I have fought the good fight, I have finished the race, I have kept the faith' *(2 Timothy 4:7)*. Somehow these sayings about races must be made to fit in with his overall attitude towards competition, which may be summed up as, 'Let each of you look not to your own interests, but to the interests of others' *(Philippians 2:4)*.

The solution, I am sure, is to regard the race as a race against myself, to get as much as I possibly can out of myself in the time left to me, to thank and praise God. My race is against the clock, not against any fellow Christian or fellow human being. The 'cloud of witnesses', mentioned in the lovely passage in the Letter to the Hebrews (12:1), may then be seen as a totally friendly and enormous crowd in the stands around the arena, willing me on to break my own personal best . . . the record previously reached by me in my own universe where I live with God. I in my turn willingly join the crowd cheering on my neighbour to greater than ever heights of service and gratitude to God, in my neighbour's arena. A famous Archbishop* once compared life to bringing home a crippled ship! Well, then, in that case I would be down at the harbour cheering home my neighbour's muddy and battered old tramp steamer, back from its world voyage, even as my neighbours and the saints of heaven have been cheering home my battered old boat.

Once I know myself as God's beloved daughter or son, unable to lose that title, then there is no further to go. I am already all that I ever will be, and all I can do is to try and live up to my title. So, no use in making it a top priority to get on in the world; no point in wanting my children to be just like me – they have their own relationship with God. 'Star differs from star in glory' *(1 Corinthians 15:41)*, and God knows each human star by name. Just as our fingerprints are different each from each throughout the world and throughout history, so any one of us can only aim at being 'the best one of me.'

No need, then, to worry and fret about 'my lifestyle', as so many do, as if it mattered terribly. In God's eyes each of us is free to live our own style, nothing to do with anyone else's, and without any need for comparisons. We have no need to be forever looking over our shoulders to see what everyone else is doing, and where they are up to and whether they are overtaking us. This is true in ordinary everyday matters and it is true in spiritual matters as well. There is no need to be keeping an eye out to see if anyone else has a better way of praying than mine, in case I be left behind in the race to be a saint. The real saints gave up that struggle long ago! By all means, if I am finding it hard to pray and to persevere in praying, then it is a good idea to look around for tips to help

---

*Archbishop Thomas Roberts of Bombay, who resigned in favour of an Indian successor and returned to England in 1949.

me keep going; but for any one of us there is no 'best' way of praying except the one that I am actually doing. Moreover, this race of mine is a marathon rather than a sprint: there is no need to do everything at once, but only to space things out and do them properly.

I used to think that the promise of the hundredfold in this life promised to anyone 'who has left house or brothers or sisters or mother or father or children or fields' for Jesus' sake referred only to those who literally gave up all their money and followed a vowed religious life. Nowadays I think rather that the promise includes anyone who is poor in spirit, anyone who is not attached to what dies but only attached to the living God. If I am fully aware of being God's son or daughter, then I can hold up my head anywhere. Wherever I go, that house is mine; wherever I stand, that land is mine. I see every man and woman to be my brother or sister; every person, man or woman, who has brought me closer to the true God, that person is my mother . . . so I have hundreds of mothers. Every man, woman or child that I have brought closer to the living God is my child, and I their mother. As Jesus said, 'Whoever does the will of God is my brother and sister and mother' *(Mark 3:35)*. And his promise is not just of eternal life in the age to come, but the hundred-fold now in this age – houses, brothers and sisters, mothers and children, and fields . . . with persecutions indeed, but these are real promises *(see Mark 10:29, 30)*.

To base my life on the truth that God loves me one-to-one and no matter what, is to be free from forever looking over my shoulder to see how everyone else is doing, and it also frees me from forever looking at the alternatives to what I am actually doing. Some people can be haunted by alternatives: the distant fields are greener, and what I am actually doing seems a bit drab. The secret, I am sure, is to carry on doing what I am doing with the best will I can muster and for the love of God, and God will let me know soon enough if there is anything else I should be doing. There is a sense in which any person of good will can say to themselves, 'I am in the right place at the right time, doing the right thing. If God wants me anywhere else, it will be made clear to me.'

The description of the average Christian at the end of life as 'a battered old tramp steamer' is usually pretty accurate, but the desire and the ambition to please God can and should be enormous within the battered hulk. God does not so much reward our performance as fulfil our desires, so it pays to keep our desires enormous. There is a strange and wonderful prayer of the Church which goes back many centuries and which ends, 'Give us in addition the things we do not dare to pray for'.*

There is a limited place for competition in education, doubtless, though it easily gets out of hand. To my mind the purpose of competition in education is to help the students to see what perhaps they too could do if they put their minds to it, and therefore to get the best out of each one. A child receiving one-to-one tutorials from one teacher would have a very restricted horizon compared with a child in a big school with plentiful resources. But the minute competition turns into a question of 'which of us is the greatest?' it becomes a menace. Jesus would have nothing to do with that question, and turned the whole idea upside down by telling his disciples instead to be like little children, giving God the glory and themselves being simply servants of God's power.

We can see so plainly the damage competition does in economics, whereby the rich get richer and poor get poorer; the First World fights to stay on top, the Second World wants to be up there at the top, and the Third World gets poorer and poorer. Yet the resources are there for everyone. Strictly speaking, none of us humans has any rights at all to wealth or property or to anything else. This is particularly true when we start fighting over blessings, since Jesus makes

---

*. . . *et adicias quod oratio non praesumit.* Prayer of 27th Sunday of the Year, formerly for centuries Prayer of 11th Sunday after Pentecost, 10th after Trinity.

it clear that if we do not forgive others, we will not be forgiven either: so the gifts are forfeit. We all came naked into
the world, every little thing in our lives is a gift, so I am no
more entitled to it than my neighbour is, nor is my neighbour more entitled than I.

Again, it seems to me, when it is a question of who came
first to a land, neither the 'original' inhabitants nor the late-
comers have any right to the land, since land is found, not
created by us. We have got ourselves into a dreadful tangle
by competition. According to Jesus we are all one family, so
why should one child in the family grasp the biggest share?
The world is Jesus' inheritance, and he is the eldest brother,
but he shares it all with us, if we look at the world as he does.
When Jesus makes his manifesto which we call the Beatitudes
(Matthew 5:1-12), two of the statements are about now, the
rest are promises for the future. 'Blessed are the poor in
spirit, for theirs is the kingdom of heaven.' Not 'theirs will
be the kingdom', but 'theirs is the kingdom'. If I can only see
the truth that everything is gift to me, then everything is mine.
Everything I can see or think or remember, all my universe is
mine, and it is filled with God. The other gift that starts now
is 'Blessed are those who are persecuted for righteousness'
sake, for theirs is the kingdom of heaven'. When others try
to take my world away because I know God's love for me,
then I have my God but nothing else; and I discover that
nothing else matters. Having my God I have everything.

The rest are promises: those who mourn will be com-
forted. They mourn over the injustices of the world, which
will be righted . . . but in God's way, since God's justice is the
same as God's mercy. The meek will inherit the earth,
because they have continued to treat the earth as a gift from
God. Blessed too those who hunger and thirst for righteousness, who long to be made right with God, and to know the
right way of looking at life. We have only to show mercy, to
find that our own burden of guilt has been lifted . . . the one
comes before the other. The pure in heart care for nothing

and nobody in place of God, and their vision grows ever clearer. Blessed are the peacemakers, peacemakers in the manner in which Jesus was a peacemaker: he taught that everyone is a child of God, not just a chosen clique. God is the great bringer of peace to the heart, so whoever is a means of that peace is in the image of God, as children are in the image of their parents.

To imagine a world without competition is wonderful, but to bring it to reality is a task big enough to last us to the end of time. However, the desires are what count in the meantime, as we pray for what we hardly dare pray for, because it seems so impossible. If the kingdom can come in my own heart, there is a chance I may be able to share it with someone else.

CHAPTER 7

The Nature of Love

The nature of love demands that love be free. The fullest story of love that Jesus gave is that of the Prodigal son, in Luke's Chapter Fifteen. Some would call it the story of the Prodigal Father who was as lavish with his love as the young boy was with his inheritance. Others call it simply the story of the missing child who came home again.

The father in the story never tried to keep his son at home. Once it became clear that the young boy wanted to break free, the father made no difficulties. Yet it is clear from the way the boy was welcomed back, that it cost the father dearly to let him go in the first place. The father saw the returning wastrel when he was still a long way off; there was no need for a servant to tell him who was coming. He must have been on the watch day after day, month after month, year after year. Nothing would seem to indicate that he only missed the youngster once he was gone: he had already made up his mind to do without him, for ever if necessary, as soon as he was asked, so as to leave his son free. Yet he was not forced to do so, not bound to do so. Of his own free will the father decided to let this youngest of his dearest treasures go, just as he would have let the first son go had he been asked.

The father freely let the son go, and it cost him dear; the son went, and it cost him nothing at the time – for him the going was free in quite a different sense. There is a freedom given, which costs the giver dearly; there is a freedom accepted and enjoyed, which costs the receiver nothing.

Then at the other end of the story, when the young man has sown his wild oats and wants to come back again, the roles are almost reversed. The son decides to take a chance on his father's tolerance yet again. Not now the chance of getting back his old place in his father's affections, he thinks; but he will go and offer himself as a servant. All the way home, that is what he has in mind. Even so he does risk rejection: it is by no means sure that his father will let him back, even as a servant. He is going back cap in hand, almost as a beggar, his pride and self-esteem badly dented, with nothing to offer except the future, and his promises. All this must have cost him dearly.

The father, on the other hand, pays nothing at all for his son's return. From his point of view, it is all gift, to have his son back. The fattened calf, the ring, the robes, the party, the musicians, none of these cost him anything, so glad is he of the return. There is in any love a first direction of love, which costs the lover dearly but which costs the loved one not at all. Then there is a second direction of love, where the roles are reversed and the loved one becomes the lover. Once the return is complete, the love is complete. In divine love, whether in God or as experienced in human beings, the Spirit of God moves first from Father to Son and then back to the Father, first from Father to child of God, then from child of God back to the Father.

In the life of Jesus, we would of course be very mistaken if we believed that his Father wanted Jesus to die a horrible death. We would be very mistaken if we thought the Father wanted any of us to die a horrible death, or even to die at all, inasmuch as death is the ultimate enemy *(1 Corinthians 15:26)*. What he anointed Jesus for was to bring good news to the poor; he sent Jesus to proclaim release to the captives and recovery of sight to the blind, and to let the oppressed go free, for that was the way Jesus himself expressed his mission (see *Luke 4:18*). It was his enemies who wanted Jesus dead, not his Father.

Why did they want him dead? They wanted him dead because they thought his teaching would lead to lawlessness and sin: if God loves the sinner and has already forgiven all sin, who would trouble to try and please God at all? 'And what about us', they would add, 'who have laboured all day and done all that God asked of us – are we to receive only the same reward as those who have done nothing, but find themselves forgiven?' Jesus on the other hand knew that when folk were forgiven with no conditions, folk like Zacchaeus or the woman who came to the meal at the house of Simon the Pharisee, the forgiven ones would respond with a generosity which in its turn had no calculation in it. Zacchaeus nearly beggared himself simply because Jesus the prophet from God treated him in a friendly fashion; the woman made a complete show of herself, washing Jesus' feet with her tears and wiping the tears away with her hair, then anointing his feet with ointment there in front of everybody, and she cared not at all who saw her or what they thought.

But Jesus' enemies are of a like mind with the elder brother in the story of the Prodigal Son: they would be just as happy if he had never come home. Their fate is not sealed, however; the father in the story tries to soften the heart of the elder son, and the story is open-ended as Jesus tells it. We are all invited to love God in return with a love which has no strings, no conditions. Whoever God wishes to forgive, let God forgive them . . . and that means everybody.

God did not want his Son to die a horrible death. God does not want our sufferings either. There are two great lessons to learn in this life: God loves us even though we are sinners, and God loves us even though we are suffering. It is quite unthinkable that a loving God would let his own children suffer needlessly. 'Love' we know from experience; 'all powerful' is beyond us. We do know that lovers do not let their loved ones suffer if there is any way round the suffering. Therefore even if God is 'all powerful', his being all-powerful cannot include the power to remove my suffering here and now, otherwise God would have removed it. God is all powerful in the way that love is all powerful: love will win the final war, even if suffering wins many of the battles along the way.

Jesus on the cross was clinging to his certainty that God loved his Son even though to all appearances everything had gone wrong. Rising from the dead he was shown, beyond the reach of suffering but otherwise very much his old self, to the chosen witnesses. Faith moves mountains, and if a mountain of suffering stands between any of us and God, then the suffering will be the first to go. God and I will still be there when the suffering has reached its time-limit and is no more.

Suffering is an evil, which love can use to demonstrate love, when there is no immediate escape from the suffering. In the nature of divine love there is always suffering of some sort along the way. When one person lets another free in the hopes that the other will come freely back home, then there is always suffering. And when the one who went away feels abandoned but still hopes against hope, of course there is suffering.

When Jesus talks about the love there is between himself and his Father, and about the Spirit, he uses these or similar terms. Jesus always wanting to do the will of his Father is to that extent always a mirror of the Father's love, and like a little child who will not cross the dangerous road without the presence of a powerful adult. Jesus flourishes under the love that comes to him from his Father, but the Father's love had no source outside of itself. Jesus is light from light, but the Father is light. The Father let go of the Son, in the hope that the Son would do what was needed, but also in the hope that the Son would not abandon hope under whatever suffering came.

The Spirit or personal relationship of love starts with the Father and goes to the Son; from the Son the same Spirit returns to the Father. In each direction the love, the Spirit of love, is freely given. Christ comes into our world bringing love with absolutely no strings, and returns to God the Father mirroring that love with no strings.

In our own lives too, the Spirit of love brought by Jesus is offered to each one of us, and all we have to do is accept it.

Faith is what justifies us, when all is said and done *(Galatians 3:16)*, faith that God really loves and forgives us without conditions. Then we are invited to give love back in return, love without conditions, so that the movement of the Spirit may be complete. The invitation to give love in return is entirely free; it has to be, or otherwise God's love would be conditional. What makes us so often put conditions on our love-in-return is the prospect of suffering. 'I loved you, God, so why did you do such a thing to me? Take it away and I will love you again.' Conditions. Yet on the one hand, God does not want the suffering, so why do I blame God? On the other hand, even if God could remove the suffering now rather than later at the best time, why do I not trust that he knows what he is about, and that he still loves me?

Little children in hospital, awaiting an operation necessary for life to continue, would easily plead with their mothers to take them out of this frightening place where there has been pain already and worse pain is expected. Yet the mother without being cruel would plead with her child to trust: she does not want the suffering, but the result of the operation will be nothing but good, and the end of pain.

CHAPTER 8

Free to Grow

I am free to grow because I am free to be less than perfect. Such will be the drift of this chapter. But to begin with, we could consider some of the images of growth that Jesus gives us.

The parables about seeds are parables about growth, as often as not. Even those which are not directly about growth are sometimes put by the evangelist side by side so as to illustrate growth. The parable of the yeast a woman took and mixed in with three measures of flour until it was all leavened, that is about growth. Really, the stories about Jesus healing people, such as I looked at in the first chapter of this book, they are about growth as well, living parables, about giving life instead of killing.

Fruitfulness is a frequent theme of Jesus', as when he complains about the vineyard tenants not giving up the fruit of the vineyard to the messengers or to the son of the owner. And Jesus looks in vain for fruit on the fig tree out of season; the evangelists hint broadly that he is really worried about the temple which looks so splendid but is unable to be everlastingly fruitful. The fig tree dies, but in the vision of the early Christians Jesus is the fruit given to God, his body and blood ever fruitful on the tree of life which the cross has become. So what has all this to do with our Christian freedom?

Quite frequently in our prayers we like to identify with one of the characters in the gospels, and to form a similar bond between ourselves and Jesus to that which the character enjoys. Some call this 'gospel contemplation'. Not so often, though, do we identify with anything other than a person in the gospels. Why not, for instance, pretend that I am the field where all this activity of growth described by Jesus takes place?

I find myself a quiet place and sit with my eyes closed. I see in my imagination a field, a space of land, and the field is me. It has no crop growing in it, at least none useful to human beings. Nowadays we do not dismiss wild flowers as 'weeds' as soon as we see them, since we have rediscovered how many healing and soothing properties may be hidden in the most ordinary wild flower. But we can take it that in my field at the start of the story there are mainly the kind of wild plants that no farmer or market gardener or flower gardener, and no chemist either, would want to be there.

The landowner and the tenant farmer come and lean over the gate at the entrance to my field. The landowner has plans, to make my barren field fruitful, and the farmer is in agreement. A desire stirs within my depths, to produce growth and become fruitful. I can dream of myself as an orchard, or a field of waving barley, or a vineyard giving a marvellous vintage. My surface may be rough and hardened by disuse, but I feel willing to let the farmer dig or plough and plant and fertilise or do whatever he sees as being needful.

So the plans go ahead: my ground is prepared and the rains water and soften me. The farmer becomes the sower, and sows the seed on my ground. In reality, the seed is the word of God, the word from God that tells me I am the beloved son or the beloved daughter. To begin with, I carry the seed lightly, but then the sower comes back over the ground to harrow it and help me take the word in deeply. The word is hidden deep in my ground for a while . . . but not so as to stay there in the dark. I puzzle over, and test, what this word could mean. I make as much room for it as I can, because it is so much better than the useless weeds that were there before.

Then this new creature, which is God's seed in my ground, comes to the surface and begins to be seen by others. I, this new creature, do not have to worry overmuch about how to grow, any more than the average child has to worry about how to grow. We just grow. My growth is not completely successful in my own eyes: some of the seed fell on stony ground, the path beside my hedge, and parts of me were still rocky underground, to say nothing of the remaining weeds and thistles that blow in from who knows where. But there is a fine crop, and the landowner is content to let me grow.

When the farmer suggests pulling out the weeds from the midst of me, the landowner is against it. I will do better if I am left free. Nobody grows happily if they are being picked on all the time. These blessed weeds are clinging creatures, and if ever any well-meaning person pulls one out, they pluck the heart out of me as well, in the sense that they make me lose heart. Whereas the landowner, contrary to all human reason, keeps on saying he is well pleased with me, and that makes me grow with a good heart.

Since I have been showing above ground, I have been the object of interest and scrutiny to the rest of the world. Here am I, claiming to be both human and divine (body, soul and spirit . . . the earth, the water, and the seed), and the rest of the world would make me conscious of my rocky ground and of the weeds that are still there. Surely I must improve and become one hundred per cent perfect before I can make any such claim? But my Father the landowner protects me, and lets me grow in peace to the harvest time.

In my full growth I can be useful to others in ways that the weeds, the thorns and the thistles, never will be. Perhaps I am so great and leafy that the little birds can find shelter in me: I tell them they do not have to be perfect before their Father will love them, just as my Father, my landowner, always told me. Or else like a field of corn or an orchard or a vineyard I can yield my fruit for the benefit of others. Some of my fruit is always kept to propagate new life, so in my turn I have become a sower like the one who sowed my field. I can only sow what was given to me, and I will never claim it as my very own.

'The divine' is what is from God. We can so easily fail to

realise what are the things that matter to God, as opposed to what are the things that matter to us. A fruitful field does not mean the same as a life that had no sins in it or no human failures in it. We have only to remember the thief to whom Jesus promised Paradise, the very same day he would reach Paradise himself. The thief admitted he deserved to be on the cross, that he deserved to be executed. To all human appearances, his 'field' was totally full of the most noxious weeds. What is more, he had no time in which to promise to clear the weeds and start again with a good crop. He was in his last hour on earth, and he made no promises: he asked only to be remembered by Jesus. Yet in divine terms that thief's final word was more fruitful than a thousand 'virtuous' lives, since it has encouraged countless millions of poor sinners to believe it is never too late to trust in God's mercy.

I am reminded of a glass test-tube: my life is like a glass test-tube. If I half fill it with wonderful deeds, God will top it up with his love and mercy. If I have no wonderful deeds at all, but still trust in God, God will fill it all the way with his love and mercy. So who is the winner? The best solution for a virtuous person is to recognise that the wonderful deeds are all God's gift anyway, and then it is still possible to be completely filled with God.

The apostles and other early disciples of Jesus grew, they did not leap full-grown into discipleship. Jesus gave many signs and exercised a lot of patience before Peter finally had his eyes opened, his ears cleared and his mouth loosened, so that he could behold Jesus as the Christ. Yet almost immediately it was as if Satan, or the birds of the air, came and snatched the word out of his mouth. That God could forgive sinners, Peter could accept; but that God could send the Messiah and still leave suffering behind in the world, that he found impossible to stomach. Then too we hear of James and John showing they were stony ground at that stage, full of enthusiasm at the start but ready to run away when persecution came and Jesus was arrested. Thorns and thistles were still there in plenty in the disciples even as Jesus went to Jerusalem for the last time, since they could not fathom how it could be difficult for a rich man to enter the kingdom of heaven and live in God's way.

There is more than one kind of 'riches'. The danger of a lot of money is that it can make the rich one indifferent to the plight of those who have little or none. The danger of a lot of 'virtue' is that it can lead the virtuous one to forget that fruitfulness comes from God alone, and belongs in God's granary. Jesus teaches, in effect, that God will forget all our weeds, if we forget all our good deeds, whereas we tend to hoard our good deeds in our own granaries.

I am free to grow because I am free to be less than perfect. Really the only way to come to understand God's love and mercy is by being free to make mistakes. Then we panic for a while, but if we are taught well we soon come to understand that mistakes are the golden way to understand the breadth of God's love. We start out thinking we are on a tightrope, but then find we have not fallen off a tightrope, but simply fallen on our faces on a broad road . . . so all we have to do is get up and carry on.

CHAPTER 9

Responsible Yet Free

God gives us humans great responsibilities, yet in the midst of them all we are still free to smile and to laugh. Laughter has been described as one of the proofs of the existence of God: if in spite of all the troubles of the world we can still sometimes laugh and often smile, it shows we are not in despair. Somewhere deep down we believe that 'all will be well in the end'. With Christians this belief is not so much deep down as near the surface. If we are each of us beloved children of God, then our ultimate peace is more assured than the movement of the stars.

The deepest truth for a Christian is that I am a child of God first, and a servant of God only in second place. I am first of all a lamb of God or a sheep in his flock, and only secondly called to be a shepherd . . . and so on down through the dozens of images given to us by the Gospels: the light must shine on me before I can reflect it to others; I must be based on the Rock before I can be a rock for others; my field must be sown with the seed before I can become fruitful; I must be shown the Way before I can show it to others. I am justified because God has adopted me as his child, not because I am a good servant.

Once we have grasped this order of priorities, then our duties and responsibilities become a joy, not an impossible burden. How could I, as a Christian pastor, ever bear the weight, if the eternal salvation of those I try to help rested on me? Much more realistic and consoling is the thought of how Jesus brought in his disciples at the feeding of the five thousand. He was the one who took to himself the role of shepherd, and who made himself responsible for seeing that the 'sheep' were fed;

but all the same he used his closest disciples. When they came to him and said everyone was getting hungry, Jesus said, 'You give them something to eat'. He made them search around to see what exactly they had to start with, and it came to five loaves and two fish. He got them to sort everyone out into companies of hundreds and of fifties: with their colourful clothing and with the green grass along the alleyways between them, they looked from a distance like flowerbeds, so St Mark tells us. Then Jesus blessed and broke the food, but gave it to the disciples to set before the people.

Jesus was the one responsible, but the disciples were learning to work with the little they themselves had, and to trust that Jesus would take it to lengths they had never believed possible. In the end they did feed the hungry people themselves, as Jesus had told them to, but it must have taken a lot of faith in him to get started with five loaves and two fish. We could take other parallel examples, like the way Jesus lets the fishermen among them fish all night without success, before getting a magnificent haul in the morning just when and where he tells them. If they had left it all to Jesus and never bothered to go out on the lake in the first place, they would certainly never have caught anything.

This balance between our small efforts and Jesus' major results runs through many passages in the gospels which might at first sight not seem to be connected with that balance. So for example where Jesus says, 'But when you give a banquet, invite the poor, the crippled, the lame and the blind' (*Luke 14:13*). Then there will be no return, since the likes of those can never afford to invite me back to their place next week for a banquet as good if not better. We can apply this principle to many situations besides those of people with physical problems. Good teachers give their lives, and yet how few are the pupils who give the teacher as much loving attention as the teacher gave them. Less skilled teachers usually suffer more than skilled teachers, and receive even less thanks for their labours. As we see with the lepers Jesus cured, about one in ten is a good score for gratitude! Parents give endless love and devotion to their little ones, and most of what they give for the first few years is completely forgotten by the children, and only comes to light when those children have little children themselves.

The secret is there in the nature of love which I looked at in the last chapter. The father of the Prodigal Son had to let go of his love, and wait as patiently as a fisherman not just for a night but for an age of nights, till the nature of divine love brought his erring son home to him. The son too could not find instant love the moment he learnt to desire it: he had to face the long walk home, travelling in hope. I myself have no children of my own, but as a pastor I have taught, cared for and loved many, from childhood up to adulthood. Yes, at least one in ten have been grateful, but there is no way anyone can force love-in-return. Love is a divine gift, and we can only work with our 'five loaves and two fishes', waiting for Jesus to turn it into a banquet.

My share of the duty as a pastor is a privilege and a joy, not a burden. My Master is not totting up my mistakes, planning to sack or disgrace me if they become too many. He has set me free from such a slavery. I am free from the need for success as a pastor, since the five loaves and the two fish are mine, but the banquet is his alone. I am free from the need for success in business or in relationships: these things do not reach to the very core of me. I am God's beloved child whether I succeed or fail, and my friendship with God is all that matters in the long run. I may 'weep now', as the Beatitude of Jesus puts it, but I will be laughing when the really important truth comes to light, that all that mattered was my trust in God.

With the Good News I am free from the need to pretend. Pretending was a trap the enemies of Jesus had fallen into. Yet why bother trying to put a good face always on everything that we ever did, saying to ourselves and to others, 'Well, I didn't do so badly, really', when it does not really matter a straw how well I did? If I fished all night in the cause of God or in the cause of myself and my family, and caught nothing, what does it really matter? Jesus is the one who decides where the catch of fish is to be found, both where and when. In the meantime I can remain cheerful, and take turns with the others in the boat to work and to relax. There is no panic.

The news that Jesus brings to my heart sets me free from regrets, since most of our regrets are about things that did not turn out as we hoped or expected. So, if all I can muster at the end of my life is 'five loaves and two fish', what does that matter? If I have given my love as a parent or as a teacher or in any other service to another, and got very little or no love in return, is that not just what Jesus told us to rejoice over? We should be glad at having in our hearts a love that does not demand a response, a love that sets others free, as does the very love of God the Father.

Looking at life in this way frees us from the need for competition, as we have already seen, since my five loaves and two fish look much the same as your five loaves and two fish, when placed against the backdrop of five thousand hungry people. Moreover, the Good News from God sets us free from the need to have praise all the time from other human beings. We have constant praise from our Father, such that each of us can say at any time and no matter how well or how badly we have just performed, 'God, I am your beloved child; you are well pleased with me'.

Lastly, I could point out that as a Christian I am free from the tyranny of time. In the context of this chapter that means I need not worry unduly about having so little time to set matters right between me and God, since they are already at rights, as a result of God's choice, not mine. I need not, as life goes on, feel I have laboured in vain, since my labour in vain is only the long night of fishing without success, which Jesus can and will put spectacularly right in a moment, leaving me laughing for ever.

There is a way of praying whereby we give our hands, our

feet, our eyes, our ears, our hearts, our tongues, our minds, our memories, all to Christ to work within us. 'Dear Lord, if you have someone you wish to attend to and I could help, here is a pair of feet: take me there. When we get there, let my eyes recognise the one. Let my ears listen, and let my tongue say the right words. Feel free to work through me: I give you full permission.' We have all of us, most likely, felt a strange rightness now and again in our lives, having arrived up at some situation not planned by us, where we said or did just the right things. As Christians we sense that Jesus took over at such times, and used us, as we had given him leave to do.

But we are not the only means Jesus has of getting through to people in distress. I must never feel that perhaps I have let some sufferer down, and that therefore they will never be helped by Jesus. I am no more than an under-shepherd, a sheep-dog more like, and the shepherd will see to the lost sheep himself if I fall down on the job (see *Ezekiel 34:11*).

To put the matter another way, the point of this chapter is to encourage us as Christians to keep going, no matter how unsuccessfully, so as to be around and still in the boat when Jesus from the shore tells us where to let down the nets. We can only do our best with the limited personal resources we have, to improve matters local, national or international along with other people of good will. If we find ourselves disheartened by how little we do, that feeling does not come from God.

CHAPTER 10

Free and Reconciled

'In Christ God was reconciling the world to himself, not counting their trespasses against them, and entrusting the message of reconciliation to us. So we are ambassadors for Christ, since God . . .' *(2 Corinthians 5:19, 20)*. The task of the Christian ambassador is to tell people they are reconciled and appeal to them to believe the message. They are reconciled, already, but they do not know it. They do not dare to believe it. These days, they are even inclined to say in reply, 'So what? I am not conscious of a need to be forgiven, by a God I do not even believe in.'

Christ was the one who brought forgiveness into the world. It was a world that believed in one God or even many gods. Jesus told those who were ready to hear it, 'Daughter', or 'son', or 'friend', 'your sins are forgiven; your faith has saved you'. That was a respectful way of saying, 'God has forgiven your sins, and blessed are you for believing it'. Jesus the ambassador was telling them the message, that they were already reconciled, could they only believe it. In one of his teachings about prayer, Jesus makes the mysterious but wonderful statement, 'So I tell you, whatever you ask for in prayer, believe that you have received it, and it will be yours' *(Mark 11:24)*. The Greek words could also mean, '. . . believe that you are receiving it, and it will be yours'. This is clearly the principle Jesus worked on with regard to forgiveness and reconciliation: he did not stop asking for forgiveness, right up to the day he died, even though he knew and taught that the forgiveness was there already.

God is and always was and always will be Forgiveness, but we only dared to believe this and act on it through the life, death and resurrection of Jesus. In his life Jesus taught forgiveness, in his death he staked his life on forgiveness, in his resurrection he was shown to be irrevocably right about forgiveness.

We have nothing to fear from God. We are like chicks under the mother hen's wings. There is a pond round the back of my house, with a pair of moorhens on it. Of a summer evening it is possible to see the chicks snuggling under the mother's wings, or later in the summer struggling still to fit under the mother's wings, as they themselves grow bigger. None of them is afraid.

We are lambs of God, cherished more than any shepherd ever cherished a lamb. God has told us as much, a thousand times over, so why do we not believe? If as lambs or as sheep we get ourselves into a tangle, feeling lost or unwanted, we are never lost to God, never unwanted by God. The shepherd will come looking for us.

We are all without exception 'first-born children', each as much loved by God as if we were the only one, with God's self and the whole universe and the whole of eternal heaven as our personal inheritance. God is not looking at our few successes or our many failures, except with compassion as we find the journey home long and tiresome.

We have only to gaze at a new-born baby and see the perfection of every little feature and finger, to know that God loves children. But God loves each of us as if we were little children, to be cherished and protected. And if a child is born handicapped or incomplete, our hearts go out to the child and its parents – so too God's heart goes out to us if we are handicapped in life or if things go wrong for us. God is not there in the handicap, but there in the love that will set all right in the end.

Jesus tells us we are like a precious coin that a woman lost, and spent ages sweeping the house out to find it again. Living in God's way is like finding a treasure in a field, and then discovering that the treasure is me, loved and sought after by

God who is the truth. Even, in God's eyes, I am a pearl of great value.

Each of us can say, 'I am the light of God's eyes'. I am God's beloved son or daughter, beloved, precious, treasured, most important to the one who is Truth itself.

'So why should we on earth be so sad, since our Redeemer made us glad? . . . when from our sin he set us free, all for to gain our liberty.' We tend to sing carols like that at Christmas, then forget the wonderful truth for most of the rest of the year. When the prophet Isaiah tells us that God is coming with vengeance, we droop our tail between our legs, so to speak, and feel guilty, when all the time Isaiah is saying that God's vengeance will be upon our enemies, not upon us: enemies like fear and envy and pain and death and hatred and despair. All these will go, and indeed they start to go as soon as we open our hearts to the glorious fact that God loves us for no reason at all. We do not have to, we cannot earn God's love and forgiveness. All we can do is ask for it.

Why ask for forgiveness, if it is ours already? For several reasons. First, Jesus told us to ask, and he never says things lightly. Second, if we stop asking, we forget eventually that the forgiveness is there, and crawl back into our fears. Third, asking reminds me that I am a creature, and it is part of my inner workings that I need to function as a creature loved from outside, who responds from inside. I am not self-sufficient. Fourth, even if my life is pretty innocuous (and isn't that a reproach in itself?) and I do not feel the need of forgiveness, there is still no relation between my life here and now, and eternal life. I cannot earn eternal life, either by being innocuous or by being a villain. I must ask for the wherewithal.

Fifth, Jesus in teaching about forgiveness and making sure we remember it every day, is revealing the most consoling truth, that reality is ultimately friendly. The singer and songwriter John Lennon told the story of how he first met his future wife Yoko Ono. He went to an art exhibition she was giving, and one of the exhibits was a 'sculpture' which involved climbing a ladder, opening a flap up there and peering through with a spy-glass. There was a word written there, and the word was 'Yes'. John was impressed: it was positive! Think of all the awful things it might have said to you, after all the trouble of climbing up there. James Joyce would have agreed with him: the last word of his great novel *Ulysses* is also 'Yes'. Ulysses and his wife come together again after their several adventures and she says, 'Yes'. What Jesus is giving us is the truth that the heart of the universe is not only saying 'Yes' but indeed 'I love you, you who are both the least of my little ones and not the least of my little ones'.

I would estimate that before the time of Jesus, the world was not yet ready to understand the key role of forgiveness. Now we are ready, but what a shame if the people of the world only discover when they die that they need not have been afraid. Just think what it would be like, to see the face of God and think, 'Oh, if only I had my time again, knowing what You are really like!' Nothing impossibly lost, in the end, but the ambassador for God is the one who tries to spread the news of what God is really like, and therefore of what reality is really like, in good time, so that people can change their ways and find real peace. The modern world may think it does very nicely without God and without forgiveness, but the modern word is not a very happy place.

I remember seeing one time on the television an extract from one of the York Mediaeval Mystery Plays. One scene in particular horrified me, because it was a travesty of real Christianity. There was a big set of scales, a balance like there used to be in the grocer's when I was a child. A see-saw, with human-size cups on either side. As each human being died, he or she was dumped into one side of the scales, and the good deeds of the person's life were put into the other side of the balance. If the good deeds were weighty enough, the angels rejoiced and away to heaven went the person. If the good deeds were too slim, or maybe it was if the bad deeds were weighty, the devil and his angels rejoiced and away to hell went the poor human creature. Where the story of the Good Thief got lost, somewhere between Jerusalem and York, I cannot imagine.

There is a beautiful Christian prayer, much older than the Middle Ages, dating in fact from somewhere like the third century of the Christian era, which entirely does away with the scales . . . but as a prayer, believing that the gift is already given. It goes like this: *Nobis quoque peccatoribus*, 'And to us sinners, your servants, hoping in the multitude of your mercies, please grant some part and share with your apostles and martyrs and all your saints. Let us into their company, not as a measurer of merit but as a generous distributor of pardon.' That notion of being weighed in the scales is so deeply engrained in the human psyche, and is the cause of so much grief in this world – grief which the news from Jesus makes unnecessary. This is why as Christians we preach Jesus' Good News, in good times, in bad times, listened to or ignored.

CHAPTER 11

Free, Still, and Everywhere

In this chapter I want to return to what I said in a previous chapter about Bishop Berkeley's ideas, but to return in more detail and at a deeper level. Any one of us, looking out through our own eyes or sensing with our own senses if we have no eyes, is aware of the world in a way that is completely special to our own self and nobody else in the universe. The only one who shares it completely with me is God. Nobody else in the whole world sees exactly what I see, modified by the quality of my eyes and from my exact standpoint. Nobody else hears exactly what I hear through my ears. The scents I smell, the tastes I taste, they are totally and uniquely mine even though others may smell or taste something very similar.

Only God and I know the exact scene, sounds, flavour of what I experience at any given moment. So too my feelings, nobody knows exactly what I am feeling at any given moment, except myself . . . and God. 'Nobody knows the trouble I feel; nobody knows but Jesus', as the song says. Whether I am really happy under my quietness, or whether I am sad under my seeming joy, others may guess, but only God and I know. I love to sit alone somewhere and think like this, 'never less alone than when alone', as John Henry Newman said. I flail around at times, wondering where God has got to, and all the time God is looking out through my eyes. The reason I cannot see God 'out there' is because God is within me, looking out through my eyes, and sharing my feelings, moment by moment.

'He who planted the ear, does he not hear? He who formed the eye, does he not see?' *(Psalm 94:9)*. And surely by the same token, he who designed our feelings, can he not feel with us? For myself, although I know the whole Trinity of God dwells within me, yet for this exercise of remembering God looking out and hearing and feeling from within me I can only manage to relate to one divine Person at any one time. Either I remind myself, 'Only you and I, Father, in the whole world, can see exactly what we are seeing at this moment'. Or else I say, 'Jesus, only you and I can see this', or else again, 'Holy Spirit, only you and I'. Somehow that places me in the same viewpoint, in the same company, with one or other of the Three, but always in the company of God.

There is an old Indian saying that the way for married couples to stay together is to love the same things together. The days of finding out about one another's past story come to an end, and the way forward is to do things together, see things together, love things together. Never mind about yesterday, today is more interesting for today, and if we share each day we need never be bored or lonely. So too between God and each one of us – not to worry about yesterday, here is today, here is God and here am I, ready to look and hear and taste and feel together whatever comes up.

One of the most helpful items I learnt in the course of studying traditional philosophy and theology was this: God is One and God is Simple. That sounds odd, but 'simple' there is a technical term. The root of the word means 'without any folds'. What it means in the case of God is that wherever God is, God is entirely there, not just partly there. What it means in my case or the case of any ordinary person, is that we cannot have part of God. So if God is within me, looking out through my eyes, then God is completely with me, not partly so. In other words, at any given moment I have the complete attention of God. God is not busy, with half a mind somewhere else in the Universe; God is completely here with me.

Even in the gospels, when we compare them with our present-day life in the Church, we can see this complete presence of God to each one. When the apostles James and John asked to sit next to Jesus in his glory, Jesus seemed to give an evasive answer, saying that such a privilege was for those for whom it had been prepared. Yet in every Communion we share with Jesus, we certainly do not sit several seats away from him. Peter at the Last Supper had to ask the beloved disciple to speak to Jesus for him, since the beloved disciple was in the place next to Jesus. We do not have to ask anyone to speak to Jesus for us at the time of Holy Communion, or indeed at any other time. Jesus is divine, and is wholly present to each one. All it needs is for us to believe the truth.

Jesus is in glory, and we can notice in the accounts of his resurrection how he is no longer tied by rules of space or time. He walks with the two disciples to Emmaus, leaves their presence, and is back to appear in Jerusalem both before they return and straight after they return. The doors may be locked in the room where the disciples were, but that does not seem to make any difference to his coming. Many people have seen him between that time and this, and always his coming is by his own choice, not in the least limited by time or space. St Paul implies that when we rise we will be like him in this respect also, having a 'spiritual body', which means a body in which the divine power is in charge. One reason there will be no tears in paradise is that there will be no need of parting from anyone we love. I can spend an eternity alone with this one and an eternity alone with that one, without ever having to say 'Goodbye' to either. Time does not come into the matter. Jesus could be totally with Mary Magdalene, totally with the two disciples, or totally with the whole gathering . . . and so shall we be able.

In a sense this is true already. Going back to the way I understand Bishop Berkeley, I can think of myself as completely still, while everything else comes to me. Our point of view about the sun, the planets and the stars has altered over the centuries, and the way it has changed can suggest a beautiful thought about our own stillness of heart. To begin with, it seemed to people that the sun went round the earth. Then Copernicus turned the point of view inside out, showing it made more sense to say the earth went round the sun. Most lately, along came Einstein to say it all depends on your point of view, since there is no fixed point in the physical universe. Earth and sun go round each other.

God is within me, and God is the fixed point who never moves. God's love will always be there for me. As far as God is concerned, I am this particular star whose name he knows, and as far as we are concerned, nothing ever changes. The stars around me each wheel round at their own pace, but at the heart of reality I never change. The rest of the universe around me is my inheritance, the universe as seen from where I stand with God.

Another image I am fond of is that of a child sitting in a cinema watching a frightening film. Sometimes the child is totally absorbed in the film, but when the story comes to the frightening bits, the child can always grip the arms of the cinema seat, look away, and say, 'It's only a story. Really I am safe and sound here in the cinema with my safe adult parents sitting beside me. Soon we shall all go home.' One of the blessings of the presence of God within us is that we can close our eyes and remind ourselves of the unchanging and loving reality which is always there and which will triumph in the end. I am not saying that real life is an illusion, only that anything that currently frightens me will come to an end; but God's love will not come to an end, and God's love is there already.

This God, who is with me in such an astonishing and intimate and total way, is just as intimately close to everyone else, and indeed to everything else, though the 'things' are not apparently aware of the fact in the way the human beings can be. Thus we can find another way of praying when we are reminding ourselves that God is within. If there is someone far away whom I am worried about, then the God who is within me is within them also. It is as though I and the one I love or worry about are really untroubled by space or time, because we are closer in love than if we were in the same room together. I used to think about this when I was at Communion and I could picture the one I was praying for as being also present at Communion; but the truth is there all the time, not just when two people are at Communion.

Some pages ago I used the phrase 'the tyranny of time'. There is also a 'tyranny of space'. Space and time, distance and separation are only tyrants if we let them be. Like so many things in our world, things the old spiritual books called 'creatures' because they were created by God but are not God, space and time are fine if we know their strengths and their limitations. We can use them in our search to please the God of love, but they can be tyrants if we let them use us.

There is a coffee mug I have kept in my room lately, which bears the message 'Remember when there was always time?' and shows an old-fashioned pocket watch with Roman numerals and hands at a quarter to twelve. I like it, because to my delight I have found that since I began reflecting and praying along the lines of this chapter there still is always time, and what is more there always will be. It is incredibly soothing to look out on the world in the company of eternal love.

CHAPTER 12

Under a Free Sky

I have a choice. I can either live my life under a blue sky, or I can live my life under a cloud. If I can believe that God, the true God, is Forgiveness, then I live under a blue sky and am warmed constantly by the sun. If I believe that the true God is 'I demand my rights', then I place myself under a cloud, and I place everyone else in sight under a cloud as well. In that case I choose a false God, and I make myself his prophet.

Perverse as it may seem, if I try to sort everyone else out, thinking to set myself free from all irritation, I end up binding myself with endless chains and tentacles. Some few people or situations may be my direct responsibility, and I have to do my best to help them find their way. But by and large, we tend to feel responsible for far too much, whereas we cannot take on the whole world. Whatever we fume about, in watching or hearing or reading the news, there is our storm cloud, because we are blaming somebody else while we tie ourselves up in frustration.

The heart of it all, and the secret of the blue sky, is that God loves each one with a parent's love; God does not eye us with the impatience of an administrator who has an untidy lot of layabouts to cope with. Just yesterday I was reading about King David's reaction to the death of his rebellious son Absalom. Absalom had been a thorn in the side of David, so that his courtiers thought David would be delighted that Absalom was no more. But then, the story goes on, 'The king was deeply moved, and went up to the chamber over the gate, and wept; and as he went, he said, 'O my son Absalom, my son, my son Absalom! Would I had died instead of you, O Absalom, my son, my son!' *(2 Samuel 18:33).*

Such a simple lament, yet it rings heartbreaking and completely true across three thousand years.

There is a forgiveness in God that is stronger than death, and that has nothing to do with how faithful we have been. The whole story of the New Testament is about God setting Jesus free as God's Son to love him in return, and then Jesus setting us free as his brothers and sisters, and then our setting one another free in our turn and bringing the rest of the world to be sisters and brothers. This goal cannot be administered into existence. Forgiveness is the only means. Christians have even in the past, though hopefully less so nowadays, tried to force non-Christians to conform to Christian ways. Clearly this has always been a contradiction in terms. We have either to love people into forgiveness, or to leave them be.

For complete freedom, it is as well to forgive situations as well as forgiving people. Forgive the past, forgive the present, leave the future to God's Providence. Forgive the past: that comes with an appreciation of the goodness of the Good News. No need to carry huge burdens from the past on my back, since Jesus says his burden is light. Everything I ever did up to the present moment has been forgiven by God, so why should I still groan under it? There may be unfortunate consequences from the past which I still have to carry, but these are never so painful once the sting of God's imagined reproach is taken away. The other day I was able to visit the Tate Gallery in London, and after looking around the whole place with its paintings and sculptures I spent an hour or two just gazing at a bright and colourful creation by Henri Matisse called by him 'The Snail'. What had been a burden, like the snail's enormous pile on its back, can become a joy, once every corner of it is covered by God's loving colours. I was completely at peace, looking at the picture of the snail, because nothing from the past was troubling me, and there was nothing to cloud the brightness of the artist's colours.

Leave the future to Providence: this is something that grows little by little out of forgiving the past. First of all the fear grows in our lives, as we begin to realise quite early on that frightening and horrible things can happen to us and to those we love. Then comes, hopefully, the realisation that God is not blaming us for anything that went wrong in the past, and that these frightening things are not punishments. Then the confidence can grow, that God is actually going through our sufferings with us – that Jesus' burden is light, so any heavy burden I find myself carrying is not of God's designing. I can either drop it if it can be dropped, or else Jesus will help me to carry it. Jesus and Simon of Cyrene carry the cross together. The end result is that I no longer fear the future in the way that I did, since the one thing that matters, namely God's love for me coming through Jesus, can never be taken away from me, no matter what happens in the future. So I can 'forgive' the future for looking threatening, rather as in the fairy tale Beauty comes to see love behind the fierce appearance of the Beast.

Forgive the present: forgive the present for not being different. I have mentioned already how the Good News can free us from always wishing we were somewhere else, doing something different. God is not sitting looking at a plan in which it says I should be in some other place! God is here.

People often worry that they are not doing very well at forgiving other folk. They pray to be able, and they try, then the very next time that person they need to forgive is mentioned or they see the face of the person, all the old resentful feelings come back. Almost certainly the best remedy is to make sure and pray for those who are my enemies, as Jesus asked us to. I cannot pray for someone without having forgiven them; so if I have prayed for them and continue to pray for them, then I can be sure I have forgiven them, no matter what my feelings may be when I next see the people in question. I need not pretend in my prayers that I have not been hurt; on the contrary, that is the main reason I am praying for them. But I can pray blessings on them, pray that they never do the like to anyone else, pray that they become gentle and forgiving in their turn . . . all these sort of things.

Forgiving is not so much a question of *doing* anything; it is more a question of *not* doing something. 'Do not judge, and you will not be judged; do not condemn, and you will not be condemned' *(Luke 6:37)*. The clear blue sky is there above us all the time, Jesus implies. If we do not bring in the clouds by judging other people, then blue is what the sky remains. Aeroplane travellers always marvel, particularly taking off from cloudy Britain in winter, that up above the clouds the sky is as blue as midsummer. In the world of our hearts, we have the option of clearing the clouds away at any time, and for ever.

There is something about the letters of John in the New Testament that has puzzled me for a long time, and I think that here is perhaps the place to try and sort it out. On the one hand, John says, 'If we say that we have no sin, we deceive ourselves, and the truth is not in us' *(1 John 1:8)*. On the other hand, he later says, 'no one who sins has either seen him or known him' *(1 John 3:6)*, meaning the sinner has never seen or known God. We are all sinners, so where does that leave us? We seem to be caught either way. Does it mean that we used to be sinners, before we came to know Jesus, but that now we will sin no more? Apparently not, since John also says that we might fall back into sin: 'My little children, I am writing these things to you that you may not sin. But if anyone does sin, we have an advocate with the Father, Jesus Christ the righteous . . .' *(1 John 2:1)*.

My instinct tells me that the answer to the puzzle lies in something I have already touched on more than once in these pages. The one who grows into God's way of thinking by listening to Jesus, that person can never be held by sin. The one who believes that Jesus is the Christ, the Son of God, believes the things Jesus said. Jesus said that forgiveness is simply *there* (the blue sky) so long as we do not start acting like false gods by condemning others.

Therefore the sinner does not remain in sin; the sinner

remains in God, under the blue sky, by getting straight up again after a fall and carrying on trying to do God's will. We are all sinners and will fall, but we can still remain in God.

One of the traditional Christian titles of Jesus is 'Key of David'. As the ancient prayer says, 'O Key of David and Sceptre of the house of Israel . . . come and lead out from the prison house the prisoner bound and sitting in darkness and in the shadow of death'. The key of David is described by Isaiah as being the key to the house of David, whose keeper 'shall open, and no one shall shut; he shall shut, and no one shall open' *(Isaiah 22:22)*. Forgiveness is the key to freedom of life, and the key to free access to the open air and the bright sky. Even at night, since night follows day in this present life, even then we can still see the brilliance of the stars.

CHAPTER 13

Freedom of Conscience

Christians believe that everyone should be allowed freedom of conscience, so in that sense freedom of conscience is not something special to Christians. 'Conscience' means here my judgement about the rightness or wrongness of the action straight in front of me. It is not what is often called conscience, namely guilt feelings about something I already did in the past. Obviously, in view of what I have been saying in these chapters, no one but God and I know whether I truly think the action in front of me is good or evil. No one else can tell me what I think is the right thing to do. No one else can tell me what I think, full stop. Even someone who claims not to believe in God has as much right as any Christian to think their own honest thoughts.

So what is special about the freedom of conscience enjoyed by a Christian? For this we need to remember what is special about being a Christian. From the beginning of this book I claimed that what makes me a Christian is hearing Jesus apply to me the words spoken by his Father to him at his baptism, so that in effect I hear: 'You, Gerald, are my beloved child; I am well pleased with you'. By the time most of us hear these words and apply them to ourselves, we are far from totally pleased with ourselves: we have often, when faced with choices, chosen the option that we knew was evil, or less good, or not pleasing to God . . . however we express it.

But the fact remains, God still believes in me, just as much as before, even if what I did in my life so far does not please him. God still loves me, in the way David loved Absalom or any father or mother loves their precious child, only more so. God is always willing each one of us, so Christians believe, to get up right away after a fall from goodness, and to try again without looking over our shoulder to see if God is after us. For a person of good will, God will never screech at them; always God's voice is gentle with those who want to please him, no matter how poor the performance may be.

And so, my conscience loves me. That is what I understand, if I am a Christian, and that is what sets me free. Jesus himself as we read of him in the gospels was always seeking to do his Father's will. He did not speak about the actual word 'conscience' as we use it, but he was speaking about conscience all the time in speaking about the need to seek the Father's will. So too for me or for any Christian: the desire to do the will of God, and my conscience, these amount to the same thing. It is always God's will and pleasure that I follow my conscience, since that is where God speaks to me about the next action I am about to perform. What my conscience asks of me is what God asks of me. And what my conscience asks of me is what my 'Abba!' asks of me, according to Jesus' way of thinking and acting. Not just a remote and distant all-seeing God, but my own first generation parent, who shares my own personal vision of the universe from where we look out together.

Now obviously this God of mine, this 'Abba!' does not love only me. Once I see myself as the temple of God, then very soon I have to acknowledge every other person in the world as a temple of God. This is the way-round that Christianity works: first to realise my own value in God's sight, and then to treat all others accordingly. My 'Abba!' is present there speaking in my conscience, and the same God is Love and Forgiveness. I am not free to come up with a conscience that involves hatred or resentment, since reality is not like that. Reality is incurably friendly and forgiving. But if I do choose badly and decide to do something evil, then my conscience, as a Christian, does not treat me like a slave, and start adding up the score against me, come the day of judgement. I am not on a tightrope. A fall is a disappointment to God and to me, but nothing has changed. Even if through habit I can no longer promise with any great hopes to avoid the temptation next time, God (my 'Abba!', speaking in my conscience) is understanding.

My conscience is not me. This is perhaps the basic difference between a Christian and an atheist, in thinking about conscience. If my conscience was me, and not the voice of another being, then my own weakness would eventually be unbearable. I do not know how atheists cope, but to me personally, that would be unbearable. I would have to resort to bluster, or to blaming somebody else, or to excuses, or to fancy arguments to justify myself, or to pretence. Either that, or to fall into despair. In my own life story, as long as I thought my conscience was me, I found my conscience to be a tyrant, because my standards did not include love and forgiveness anything like enough: what I demanded was perfection. Much the same happens if I equate my conscience with the voice of God, but do not see God as being the 'Abba!' kind of God. I then make God in my own image and likeness, ignoring Jesus' basic message, and end up with a tyrant just the same as before. Yet another false god and false tyrant is the one that says my priority is to live up to other people's expectations.

In the gospel story, the clearest illustration of the way Jesus points up the real nature of conscience is the incident concerning Zacchaeus *(Luke 19:1-10)*. Zacchaeus was a villain, a tax collector, an extortionist and a cheat. Jesus saw him perched in the branches of a sycamore tree, trying to get a better view of this prophet from God. And the prophet from God, instead of shaking his fist at Zacchaeus or denouncing him, says in a perfectly friendly way, 'Zacchaeus, hurry and come down; for I must stay at your house today'. Jesus, for that moment become the conscience of Zacchaeus, was incurably friendly. And the result was that the tax collector was able to begin his life all over again from that moment, becoming not just decent and law abiding, but extremely generous: 'Look, half of my possessions, Lord, I will give to the poor; and if I have defrauded anyone of anything, I will pay back four times as much.'

The Christian conscience leaves people free to love, free to be generous. It also saves the poor sinner: the Good Thief, at least at the end of his life, believed in the forgiveness of sins. He forgave Jesus for not getting him down from the cross, did not blame Jesus for anything, and asked for forgiveness. Forgiveness is what he got, and a promise of Paradise the same day as Jesus would reach there.

Jesus gave us the climax of truth about conscience. There had been a long growth in understanding over the preceding centuries, and Jesus was not just the natural outcome of that growth: he represented a leap that no one could have anticipated or dared to expect. In the early days of the Bible story we see Abraham coming to understand that God did not want human sacrifice. First he understood that God wanted the sacrifice of his son Isaac, then he was given to understand that God did not want that sacrifice. Faced with seeming contradiction from God, Abraham chose to believe the second message, which must have been a 'still small voice of calm' compared with the strident shock of the first message. To this day we are safer following the gentler voice within us, in questions of doubt as to what we should do.

Nearer to the time of Jesus, the prophet Jeremiah said there would be a new covenant, and the law of God would be written on our hearts. We would not need to turn to anyone else to ask about how to know the Lord: we would each be on familiar terms with God. Jeremiah and the other later prophets who promised a new covenant were coming to the conclusion that God had been so forgiving, time after time and century after century, that the covenant of Moses was somehow inadequate to express the fullness of God's love and mercy. What the new revelation would be, they could not guess, but they could sense it coming.

Jesus turned morality and conscience upside down. Instead

of 'Love God and then God will love you', Jesus teaches that God loves us incurably, so what are we going to do about such generosity? Conscience is the voice of somebody – yes. Conscience is the voice of somebody absolutely perfect – yes. But perfection equals forgiveness, perfect forgiveness. So conscience is the voice of somebody who loves us for no reason at all on our side, with unconditional love.

St Paul tells us, 'There is no longer Jew or Greek, there is no longer slave or free, there is no longer male or female; for all of you are one in Christ Jesus' *(Galatians 3:28)*. What with the racial tensions that still flourish, the political injustices that still exist, and the unfairness dealt out to so many women, there is still plenty for consciences to do. But we tend to forget that in our heart of hearts we have to forgive people for doing what they are doing, before we can expect them to leap into generosity like Zacchaeus.

CHAPTER 14

Free from Fear of Death

A certain amount of fear of death is good and natural. Nobody should want to go to pieces, and a healthy desire to stay alive can prevent us from doing foolish or dangerous things with our precious lives. Also we know from experience that not all deaths are peaceful and pleasant, quite the contrary. But religious teachings can double and more than double that needful fear of death, the teachings of Christianity included, unless we understand the teachings correctly. Human nature seems to be only too ready to fear the worst, as to what might happen to us when we die. If there is a stern meaning that can be given to a doctrine, that is the meaning most folk will go for, in my experience.

One of my happiest memories as a writer concerns an old man who was dying of cancer, and who was terrified of dying. He was a Christian, and someone gave him one of my books to read, the one called 'Abba! Father!'. The family told me afterwards, he read the book avidly, and then said, 'Ah, well, if that is what God is like, I don't mind dying at all'. After which in due course he died very peacefully.

But often it happens that when I tell people about the Good Thief, they counter with 'But what about the sheep being divided from the goats?' It depends where you start: either Jesus has two faces, or one is the true face and the other I have misunderstood. Jesus welcomed the thief into Paradise at the end, but if a year or two earlier that same thief had asked Jesus what he should be doing with his life, Jesus would have told him the story of the sheep and the goats, about feeding the hungry and clothing the naked and welcoming the stranger, and 'Just as you did it to the least of

these who are members of my family, you did it to me.'
Right, but the Jesus on the cross is saying, in effect, 'Well, you
never did those things. But you are asking for forgiveness
now, and I give it to you.'

Panegyrics make me nervous. If some good person dies,
and then the preacher at the funeral service goes on about
what a wonderful person this was, as full of good works as
Dorcas *(Acts 9:36-43)*, and *therefore* sure to go straight to
heaven, then I get quite upset. The implication is, that the
rest of us, being not so full of good works (a good half of the
congregation will put themselves in this category, especially
since this may be the first occasion for some time they have
shown their faces in church) are not really in the running for
Paradise.

I was taught as a church student that the mark of baptism
is that it gives the baptised one a place at the table of God.
Your place, my place, and the place of any person baptised
in water or in desire, is fixed at the table in heaven. So long
as I am willing to sit there with whoever else God has placed
to right and left of me, there I belong. The rest of life is my
'Thank You' to God for saving a place for me. We are justified
by our faith in God's love for each of us, and our good works
are an attempt to thank God for the gift; they are not to be
confused with the thing that justifies us.

Here again, many people to whom I tell this make difficulties: 'What about Hitler? Does that mean everybody goes to
heaven?' People who are huge objects of hatred are I think a
distraction to following the truth about salvation, though I
have come across a surprising number of old men and old
women who secretly confide that they pray for Hitler and
other major sinners of history quite a lot. Broadly speaking,
no matter what shape we turn up to heaven in, God our
Father will welcome us home, but then the first sight apart
from God we shall see on going through the gates will be the
very person or persons we have never been able to stand.
Then our choice will be like that of the elder brother in the

story of the Prodigal Son: forgive and stay, or harbour hatred and go someplace else. In the meantime it will pay us to pray earnestly for our enemies, as a token of our desire to forgive them.

We are all rich in the gifts of God, even if some are more gifted than others. Even those who rail against God have the gift of a mind and body to rail with. Even those who are handicapped by human standards have some precious possessions. Death is like the eye of the needle in Jesus' illustration, the impossibly small opening we all have to go through before reaching eternal life. In the natural, healthy turn of events, people grow old and lose their gifts one by one. Sometimes they are glad enough to be without them, when the time comes at last. Grandparents find that the grandchildren are somehow a lot more exhausting than their own children ever were. Teachers, even those who loved teaching, are often happy enough to retire: conditions are not as easy as they seemed in the early days of teaching. Car drivers are often content to leave the driving to someone else, once they reach a certain age. Mobility becomes more difficult, but the old are often glad enough to stay put and welcome everyone else who wants to visit them: the dearest friends are usually the ones who will make the effort. In the end, as Shakespeare wryly put it, we find ourselves 'sans eyes, sans teeth, sans taste, sans everything'. When we find ourselves completely naked, with everything gone, then we are in the right frame of mind to meet our creator and be clothed again, on a different footing from before. By then we will know that everything, just everything, was a gift all along.

Jesus assured us, 'Do not judge, and you will not be judged'. If, as part of our Christian life, we try not to judge others, and if we are praying for our enemies, then there is no need to fear the judgement. It is not part of Christian life to be going through life looking over our shoulders, watching our backs. I myself am at an unfair advantage in this respect, since many years ago I had a dream which I have always regarded as a vision, in which I came to my moment of judgement in great trepidation and was simply embraced and hugged by Jesus wordlessly, and sent back to keep on doing my best, no matter how flawed my best might be. I have never been afraid of the other side of death ever since.*

We cannot be original without being lonely. One of the aspects of death that makes it like the eye of a needle is the fact that we can only fit through one at a time. We might die alongside someone else, just as we might have been born in the same hospital ward with someone else. But the actual being born and the actual dying we do alone. On the other hand, we like to think of ourselves as living a unique life, with our own fingerprint on our own particular story. We like to think that we have a contribution to make to the history of the world, such that things would not be quite the same had we not chanced along. My point is, we cannot have the one without the other. If I were not alone, the contribution would not be mine alone; any event would be just vaguely 'ours' without any spot within it being the bit that I did.

The picture I find most helpful here is that of a jig-saw puzzle. There it is, perhaps, a jig-saw with a thousand pieces, and I come to the very end of it and find there are only nine hundred and ninety-nine pieces in the puzzle, because who-ever pieced it together last time lost one when they put it away carelessly in the box. Now it does not matter where in the picture on the puzzle my one missing piece belongs: it could be something very special like the tip of the heroine's nose, or it could be totally obscure like a bit of blue sky or a bit of green tree-top. Wherever it was supposed to fit, the whole puzzle is marred without it. So too with ourselves: my life may be insignificant in my own eyes, but the whole pic-ture will be marred without me, just as much as if somebody desperately important went missing. Jesus tells us how a

*The story is told in my *The Other Side of the Mountain* (Geoffrey Chapman, 1989).

woman swept her whole house out looking for a missing drachma; we ourselves have probably searched the house out for a missing piece of jig-saw puzzle in our time. That piece of puzzle is unique.

One of the ways we tend to use the thought of our death is not always useful. There are good ways, like when facing an important decision I might think to myself, 'When my days are at an end, what will I then wish I had done now?' And then, hopefully, to follow the choice that will lead to less regrets. But there is a way of thinking about death that is not helpful. Very often it involves choices about sex, or worries about sex. 'Here I am, at a certain age in my life, and I have never been totally fulfilled/never had any children/never found a partner who could stay with me for life/never experienced love to the full'. Then the next thing is either to fall into depression or to do something stupid. What I say about the jig-saw puzzle may sound trite, but I am deadly serious: my real value may be something quite other than the dreams I am pursuing more and more hopelessly. We always under-estimate the strength of the urge in nature to keep our species going, linking it with this person or that person when the urge in itself is impersonal. Besides which, fruitfulness is not just a thing to leave behind in the form of children, but is something we take with us beyond death.

I like to think that even if there were no after-life, I would still prefer to have lived this life trying to reflect a loving God, rather than live a life of greed. I would far rather own the whole universe than just grasp my own little corner.

CHAPTER 15

Deliver Us from Evil

Every Christian probably prays, 'Deliver us from evil' at least once a day, as part of the Lord's Prayer. Once again we remember Jesus' saying, 'Whatever you ask for in prayer, believe that you have it, and it will be yours'. This surely is one of the prayers that is bound to be answered.

There are two main kinds of evil. There is the kind that means no harm: even an earthquake means no harm, since there is no personal malice behind it. Then there is the personal hatred that means us evil, and that is the real evil. In different ways believing in Christ delivers us from both kinds of evil.

In what way does being a believing Christian free us from such evils as earthquakes, floods, falling buildings and the like? Chiefly by reassuring us that God is not deliberately aiming these horrors at us. It is quite unthinkable that my 'Abba' would do that kind of thing on purpose to hurt me, so whatever the explanation, it is not malice on God's part. There is also the clear hope that when this earthly pilgrimage is over, there will be no more tears. After all, the very words 'Deliver us from evil' rather presume that we are already in the middle of evil, wanting badly to get out.

Then how does being a Christian deliver me from the evil intentions of my enemies? Partly in ways that I have already suggested: if I am conscious of inheriting the whole universe, then the petty desires of someone else to take away my goods or even my life are seen as petty and to be pitied, since my enemies run the serious risk of getting what they desire and nothing else in this life or the next. Then there is the deep conviction that my enemies are missing the truth: they may accuse me of all sorts and shut themselves out of God's pity, whereas I have only to forgive them and my sins no longer matter on the eternal level. Jesus says I am already blessed when others persecute me for believing in him. I do not even have to plan how to answer my accusers, since the Holy Spirit will answer for me.

But there are other ways of looking at the evils of life that I find take the sting out of much of it. One way is to think of my life as a symphony still being written, with its tranquil movements and its turbulent ones, its charming passages and its rough surprises. When my life is over the symphony will be complete, as it would be complete on paper in the composer's studio. There still remains the playing of my symphony and your symphony and the glorious tale of the lives of all those I love and admire, and indeed the symphonies of every creature that ever lived under the sun, played by the full orchestra, as many times as we wish to hear them. And because the music is complete and has come to a true conclusion, the hearing of it in all its endless complexity and richness will give endless joy. There have been a million things in my own, one, life which I would dearly love to know the ultimate meaning of; how much more, to see how God brings all to a triumphant conclusion.

There may be passages in our lives we would wish to cut out from any symphony to be heard in public, and I am sure God will respect any such wish on our part; but the strange result of God's forgiveness is that it makes our very sins more like discords delightful in the resolving of them. One of the early Fathers of the Church compares our sins to wounds inflicted in the battle of life, so that our Captain is not ashamed of them, nor of the risks taken on his behalf which they imply. Of course, I am meaning here the ways in which heaven can make sense of the pain of this world: as well as that there will be in heaven limitless opportunities for new life and new joys, not in any way chained to what happened here.

Again, my life, and anyone's life, is like a black and white film from the 1930s which I know will have a happy ending. I will never forget being taken as a boy of ten to see John Gielgud playing Shakespeare's Hamlet in a Manchester theatre. There was a spare seat because someone had dropped out of the party, so my parents debated whether I was old enough, and in the end took me along. Complete dismay at the end of the play, when there were about nine dead bodies strewn about the stage and only one walking wounded. 'Is that the *end*?!!' I was used to books like Biggles and films that had happy endings for the good people.

The greatest reassurance of being a Christian is a belief in the resurrection. Jesus rose triumphant over death; Jesus was therefore right in God's eyes, and his God and my God really is 'Abba' such as Jesus described. Also, Jesus promised Paradise to those who were willing to accept it as a gift as well as to forgive everyone else, so Jesus must have been right about that too. Therefore, all will be well. I am living through a film with a happy ending. The heroes and the heroines and all the good people may be going through all sorts of troubles and disasters, but in the end it will all make sense. That may sound trite, but I am sorry if it does, because I believe totally in the happy ending.

One of the things I find myself saying to parents who are deeply concerned about their children going off the rails or not conforming to the expectations of the previous generation: 'All will be well in Paradise, and you have been promised a new life with no tears. If your children were not there with you, it would be tears all the time, isn't that so? In that case, they will have to be with you. If you can forgive them, as I know you do, then surely God can and will, since God's mercy is infinitely greater than yours.' We have to forgive ourselves as well as forgiving everyone else. Parents can so easily interpret their children's independent way of going on as being somehow their own fault as parents.

Sometimes of course the evil is inside our own selves. We find ourselves stuck with a bad habit like smoking or losing our temper or being too quick to judge other folk. The first step to a cure is to forgive ourselves, since God has already forgiven us. Then there are simple means we can take to lessen the damage we do: one remedy is simply to count up at the end of each day how many times we have fallen down on the special habit we wish to cure, and make a discreet note of the number. Just doing that day by day and comparing week by week, month by month, can have a remarkable effect. It is a method I learnt as a young man, then abandoned, but have now returned to with gratitude, because it works. Probably the difference is, that now I start out knowing that God has forgiven what I am doing, even before I begin to try and heal it.

I have written elsewhere (*Finding the Still Point*, Eagle, 1993) about my belief that human nature is good, but good so long as it is doing what it was created for. We all have a still point within us where evil cannot touch us; but we tend to sway to one side or the other, down towards depression or up towards panic or over-excitement. Then we can no longer see straight, and we get ourselves into trouble, and usually complicate the lives of a lot of other people as well. The human evil in the world is the result of all the tangles that come from countless generations getting out of kilter with themselves. My 'still point' is doubly a gift from God: I can call myself God's beloved child, loved by God with a love that is in some way unique to me, and I have my invitation from God to love others in that same unique way.

I am not free to love unless I am free *not* to love. I suppose that is the real paradox, which I have been looking at in these pages. The only way I could be free *not* to love God is for God to continue to love me all my life even if I never loved God back. And without threats. 'Love me or I will punish you for ever' is no kind of freedom. We find this total freedom hard to understand, but once understood it lets us into the mind of Jesus. He had total freedom and knew it, but did not cling to his total freedom; he put it to one side and acted like a servant of God instead of like an everlast-ingly beloved Son. Total love gives total security, to take risks and serve and trust. It is good to be free enough to get up from my place at the table and serve others, confident that my place will be still kept for me when I return to it. It is good to give other people the total security I enjoy, by not judging them either.

I was struck one time by a senior churchman I heard, talking in conversation, saying how he was jolly well looking forward to the reward he personally was due for having put up with so much for the Lord. What a pity to set one's sights so low, I thought at the time. I would much prefer to have the same as everyone else, namely the whole universe, the new heaven and the new earth and all the love there is, without having deserved it at all.